T0271101

Organizational Constitution in Entrepreneurship

This book presents the seven entrepreneurial activities (SEA) model of new organizational constitution, a prescriptive extension of the four flows model tradition of communicative constitution of organizations (CCO) theory.

Organizational Constitution in Entrepreneurship explains the SEA model in detail, illustrating it with autobiographical accounts from Deanna Bisel's years of experience as an entrepreneur. The volume explores how entrepreneurial efforts to create and maintain organizations involve interrelated activities. In doing so, it offers a vision of new organizational creation and maintenance as (a) communicative and material, (b) initiated by value propositions, (c) difficult to achieve, (d) having periods of partiality, (e) being the result of constitutive leadership distributed among members, and (f) dependent upon constitutive momentum generated in organizational learning.

This unique volume will be a key reference for students and scholars of organizational communication, management, business studies, entrepreneurship, and communication studies.

Ryan S. Bisel (PhD, University of Kansas, USA) is Professor of Organizational Communication in the Department of Communication at the University of Oklahoma, USA. His works are published in communication and management journals, such as *Management Communication Quarterly, Academy of Management Journal, International Journal of Business Communication, Journal of Applied Communication Research, Leadership Quarterly, Human Relations, Communication Monographs,* and *Small Group Research.* His book, *Organizational Moral Learning: A Communication Approach* (Routledge, 2018), was honored with top book awards from two Divisions of the National Communication Association. His research interests include leadership communication and behavioral ethics.

Deanna L. Bisel (BBA, Washburn University, USA) is a retired entrepreneur and current philanthropist. She founded a Minuteman Press franchise in Lawrence, Kansas, USA. Her company was inducted into the President's Million Dollar Circle by Minuteman Press International and recognized by *Small Business Magazine* as one of the 25 Best Companies Under 25 Employees in the Kansas City area. She has been recognized as a business and community leader with such awards as Junior Achievement Business Hall of Fame, Washburn University Distinguished Service Award Recipient, ATHENA Award for Excellence in Mentoring Women, Sam Walton Business Leadership Award, and American Business Women's Association's Woman of the Year.

Routledge Studies in Communication, Organization, and Organizing

Series Editor: François Cooren

The goal of this series is to publish original research in the field of organizational communication, with a particular—but not exclusive—focus on the constitutive or performative aspects of communication. In doing so, this series aims to be an outlet for cutting-edge research monographs, edited books, and handbooks that will redefine, refresh and redirect scholarship in this field.

The volumes published in this series address topics as varied as branding, spiritual organizing, collaboration, employee communication, corporate authority, organizational timing and spacing, organizational change, organizational sense making, organization membership, and disorganization. What unifies this diversity of themes is the authors' focus on communication, especially in its constitutive and performative dimensions. In other words, authors are encouraged to highlight the key role communication plays in all these processes.

For a full list of titles in this series, please visit www.routledge.com.

Speaking with One Voice
Multivocality and Univocality in Organizing
Edited by Chantal Benoit-Barné and Thomas Martine

Communicating Authority in Interorganizational Collaboration
Rebecca M. Rice

The Routledge Handbook of the Communicative Constitution of Organization
Edited by Joëlle Basque, Nicolas Bencherki, and Timothy Kuhn

Organizational Constitution in Entrepreneurship
Movable Type
Ryan S. Bisel and Deanna L. Bisel

Organizational Constitution in Entrepreneurship

Movable Type

Ryan S. Bisel and Deanna L. Bisel

 Routledge
Taylor & Francis Group

NEW YORK AND LONDON

First published 2023
by Routledge
605 Third Avenue, New York, NY 10158

and by Routledge
4 Park Square, Milton Park, Abingdon, Oxon OX14 4RN

Routledge is an imprint of the Taylor & Francis Group, an informa business

British Library Cataloguing-in-Publication Data
A catalogue record for this book is available from the British Library

ISBN: 978-1-032-25746-4 (hbk)
ISBN: 978-1-032-27091-3 (pbk)
ISBN: 978-1-003-29131-2 (ebk)

DOI: 10.4324/9781003291312

Typeset in Times New Roman
by codeMantra

In loving memory of Ronald G. Bisel—husband, father, grandfather

—Dee, Kristi, and Ryan

Contents

Acknowledgments

We are grateful to our family, friends, colleagues, employees, co-workers, and customers.

From Ryan: I wish to thank my wife, Adele, for giving the book its subtitle and for her constant support throughout the writing process. Also, I am grateful to my sister, Kristi, for her valuable feedback on aspects of several chapters. I wish to thank Dr. Michelle Shumate, Dr. Keri Stephens, and Dr. Stacey Connaughton for their valuable feedback on an early iteration of the ideas presented in Chapter 2. Their encouragement and keen insights helped make the SEA model a reality. Similarly, I wish to thank Dr. Joel Iverson for his encouragement and thoughtful feedback at the outset of our conceptualization of this book. Additionally, I am deeply grateful for the sophisticated writings and thinking of Dr. François Cooren and Dr. Robert McPhee, whose brilliance in crafting two traditions of CCO over the past 25 years provides a rich intellectual heritage for the modern study of organizational communication.

From Dee: I wish to thank my late husband, Ron, who excelled in love, listening, hard work, and in encouraging me to take calculated risks. His influence is seen throughout my stories presented in this book. It was great fun to collaborate with our son, Ryan, on this book. Many thanks to our daughter, Kristi, who was my proofreader and memory jogger. Thanks to both of you for this amazing opportunity to work together, laugh together, recall memories, and make new ones. I would like to extend a special thank you and recognition to the amazing team at Minuteman Press: Sherrie, Dorothy, Eric, Ken, Jim, Kristel, Linda, Brian, and Seth. You deserve the credit for my stories (the good ones!) and the success of our business. To my ATHENA sisters whose experiences, wisdom, and character are woven into the pages of this book. Thank you! Also, thank you to Bonnie Lowe and her staff at the Lawrence Chamber of Commerce for their support of local small businesses and helping us with our success and growth. Finally, I wish to give a special thanks to the late Les Krull, who was my mentor, coach, and friend. He taught me that employees are any organization's greatest asset, that true leaders lead by example, and that true character is what you do when no one is looking.

1 CCO Theory, the Four Flows Model, and New Organization

Abstract

In this chapter, foundational ideas of communicative constitution of organizations (CCO) theory are explained. Then,
the four flows model (FFM), which is one specific tradition
of CCO, is described in greater detail. CCO theory states
that communication makes organizations what they are. The
FFM explains that organizations themselves come forth when
and where the communication flows of activity coordination,
self-structuring, membership negotiation, and institutional
positioning mix over time and space. Six basic premises of
the FFM and three addendums related to material resources
are also covered. The FFM has an intuitive fit for explaining how new organizations can be created and maintained.
Yet, to date, the model has mainly been used to explain how
organizations decline. The chapter serves as a springboard
from which to understand the seven entrepreneurial activities
(SEA) model of new organization creation and is designed to
stimulate crosstalk between the fields of communication and
entrepreneurship.

Communication can make or break a new organization. We have all
heard and told stories of those times when an entrepreneur's sales
pitch sealed the deal, a boss's fair and caring approach supported
employees' satisfaction and reduced turnover, or an employee's extraordinary customer service made her a fixture of the company
and community. Stories of how good-quality communication can
"make" an organization are commonplace in discussions of the
workplace. Meanwhile, the opposite seems to ring true: We have
heard and told stories of how a boss's abuse de-motivated employees, an employee's poor service undermined customer confidence,
or a team's silencing of a dissenter resulted in misguided plans.
Indeed, stories of how poor-quality communication can "break"

DOI: 10.4324/9781003291312-1

an organization seem all too easy to find. Perhaps these truths are especially relevant when discussing the creation of a *new* business organization.

This book asks the question, "What if these kinds of statements were more than just sayings?" What if communication makes organizations *what they are*? If that is the case, understanding communication provides a window into the animating forces and lifecycles of entrepreneurial efforts that require the establishment of a new organization. But is communication too small and fleeting to have such a big influence? Thinking of communication as the animating force of an organization requires a sensitivity to the reality that small inputs can have big outputs. Take, for example, a long-term, happily married couple. A strong relationship is a big and enviable output. Yet, research demonstrates that marriage relationships are the sum of the daily interactions that make them what they are.[1] Day-to-day talk, fun, flirting, occasional deep conversations, and, yes, even productive conflict all add up to the quality of *the* marriage relationship. Daily exchanges link, amplify, and recur over expanses of time to become the significant outcome of marriage. In much the same way, this book explores the varied ways that entrepreneurial communication activities link, amplify, and recur—in good and bad ways—to determine the life and death of organizations and especially of new business ventures that require the establishment of an organization.

This book explores the implication of communicative constitution of organizations (CCO) theory for the activities of entrepreneurs and vice versa. CCO theory is a widely accepted idea in the modern academic field of communication, and it suggests that organizations are themselves made up of, or called into being by, communication processes and material conditions.[2] We discuss the theory in the following pages, but for now, consider the observation that new business ventures tend to have short lifespans and are difficult to maintain.

Survival rate statistics of new small businesses make the point: U.S. Bureau of Labor Statistics suggests that roughly 20% of small businesses will not survive the first year; 30% will not survive the second year. Half of all small businesses will fail before 5 years in existence and 70% of small business ventures fail within a decade.[3] Clearly, small business survival is neither easy nor a given. These statistics can (unfortunately) be used to discourage or de-motivate would-be entrepreneurs, but that is not our goal. The general pattern of small business survival suggests that the *momentum* needed to create and maintain organizations is difficult to generate.

CCO theory can help to explain why that momentum is difficult to create but also exactly what communication and material issues must be addressed to get an organization moving forward and keep it running. In the following pages, we explain CCO theory in detail and lay out its premises and addendums. The purpose of this explanation is to provide a necessary background upon which we will describe a prescriptive extension of CCO theory, namely, the seven entrepreneurial activities model of new organizational constitution, or the "SEA model" for short (see Chapter 2 for details).

A Brief History of CCO Theory

CCO theory was named around 2009.[4] However, organization scientists worked with the idea for at least three decades prior to that time. The main idea of the theory is that organizations can appear stable and static in retrospect, but, in reality, are in constant need of being reproduced in interactions. Imagine, for example, a local, family-owned automotive shop. What if the owner and main skilled mechanic became ill and could not service work orders? If the shop cannot complete customers' requests and obtain the money that sustains the company, then the organization itself would also cease to exist, sooner or later. The transactional communication of requests and money into and out from the shop comes to be the animating force of the company itself. In this way, the organization must be reproduced via interactions often; otherwise, decline is inevitable and can be quick.

However, surely we would ask, Aren't small businesses different than a major multinational organization?: The answer seems to be, yes and no. Yes, because major multinational organizations have staying power afforded by a lot of legitimacy, members, materials, and capital, which have been built up over time. No, because even large organizations can fail in their ability to reproduce themselves when they are unable to communicate well enough inside and out to avoid declining—and decline can happen in a surprisingly rapid fashion. Consider, for example, the hundred-year-old Hertz rental car company. The coronavirus pandemic meant travel came to an unexpected standstill in late March 2020; the market for rental cars ended overnight. By the end of May 2020, Hertz filed for bankruptcy.[5] Its half a million rental cars and hundreds of locations around the world meant that the organization needed constant reproducing through transactions and communication with customers. On the other hand, the sheer volume of goods, facilities, and members meant that Hertz's materials (e.g., rental cars) and brand name would not fade as fast; the momentum of a hundred years helped in some ways, but not others. Yet, the point remains that organizations are not merely buildings and stuff; the animating force of communication and material resources are essential to survival.

A major starting point in the history of CCO theory involves the pioneering work of Karl Weick, professor of social psychology. Weick had an uncanny way of seeing organizations for what they really are. Weick proposed that organizations are interpretation systems in that in every organization—no matter how big or small—people need to make sense of the organization's situation and make decisions accordingly.[6] Should we hire new employees? Should we invest in a marketing campaign? Should we lease more equipment? The list of questions to decide upon goes on and on, but the questions are not always and only of the kind that executives figure out. Employees at every level of the organization are also making sense of their work and situations they face. Employees are making sense of questions, such as: Should we obey all the policies or are some policies more flexible than others? Am I being paid fairly, or do I need to even score in another way? Should I stay or should I go?

Weick's genius was to see all this communication activity and sensemaking swirling around among executives, managers, frontline employees, vendors, and customers (and back again!). Questions and answers, situations, and interpretations fill hallways, offices, parking garages, shared commutes, common areas, private areas, and board rooms. Taken together, all that sensemaking means organizations are themselves interpretation systems.[7] They must be, because organizations cannot *do* anything without people who communicate to make sense of the world around them and then act according to that sensemaking.

In the following decades, organizational communication scholars were inspired by these ideas and wrote many books and articles. Scholars were attempting to answer several key questions about communication's relationship with organization, but they had in common the notion that communication makes organizations what they are. The aptly titled book, *The Emergent Organization*, was published at the turn of the century and was influential in academic circles and established a conceptual foundation for what would later become known as communicative constitution of organizations theory, or "CCO theory," for short.[8]

Words, such as *constitution or constitutes*, can seem odd; yet, we use the word in everyday speech. Think of it this way: Nations have *constitutions*—those defining documents that declare the nation-is-a-nation and outline power distributions and rules for the exercise of that power. Not just any document can succeed in calling a nation into being. It must be signed by the "right" individuals under the "right" geopolitical circumstances and acknowledged as legitimate by other nations. However, the insight here is that a document—a piece of communication—calls a new social reality of collective action into being. Sure, a continent of South America exists regardless, but the nation of Brazil is called into being by its constitution. That whole communication process of the founding of a nation is a close analogy to CCO theory. Of course, this example is just another reminder of the incredible power of communication to create significant social realities that we can so easily take for granted after the fact.

As often happens, the CCO theory literature is fragmented into a few schools of thought: the Montréal School, the Niklas Luhmann School, and the FFM. Descriptions of the differences among all three of the CCO schools are available elsewhere.[2] A main difference is about whether *non*humans (e.g., computers and office buildings) have agency and whether nonhumans can accurately be characterized as contributing to the constitution of organization. For the purposes of this book, we focus on the FFM version of CCO theory.

The FFM

The FFM of CCO theory offers a specific answer to the question, "*What kinds of communication* makes organizations what they are?" Rather than merely making the abstract claim that communication makes organizations what they are, the FFM tells us which kinds of communication make organizations what they are. In doing so, the model gives us an opportunity to see communication examples and conversational moments that show how the CCO claim works in actual practice.

The FFM was proposed by Robert McPhee and Pamela Zaug in the year 2000.[9] The model was inspired by Anthony Giddens's (1984) structuration theory.[10] McPhee and Zaug were influenced by Giddens's arguments that attempted to settle an old debate: Namely, scholars debated whether all human behavior is determined in advanced by social structures (e.g., institutions, national cultures) or are humans free to act outside of those structures? The debate is a close parallel to the fate-versus-free will, Calvinism-versus-Arminianism clashes.

Giddens resolved the dispute by directing attention toward how these dynamics really unfold over *time*. His structuration theory states that—on one hand—individuals can, indeed, act in opposition to the structures of their social world. On the other hand, as individuals act, they produce and reproduce the social structures that will inevitably influence their future choices. In other words, "chicken-or-the-egg." For Giddens, social structures emerge from within humans' actions and vice versa.

McPhee and Zaug adopted those ideas and took them into the domain of organizations and their communication.[9] The scholars reasoned that the relationship between organizations and communication is structurational. That is to say that as humans communicate (in specific ways), they produce and reproduce the social structure of "organization." The organization, then, inevitably influences their future communication and behavioral choices. Some readers will find it easy to see organization as static, monolithic, and *prior to* communication. Others will find it easy to see organization as fluid, dependent upon, and *originating in* communication. McPhee and Zaug apply Giddens's logic and suggest that both views are correct, we need only see the relationship unfolding over time.

McPhee and Zaug specified the communication types that come to make organizations what they are. The model explains that the communicative constitution of organizations arises where two or more of the following four kinds of communication are occurring across time and space; specifically, those flows include activity coordination, self-structuring, membership negotiation, and institutional positioning. We unpack each flow in the following paragraphs.

Activity coordination. Activity coordination refers to the meaning-making of working together with another or others. When we work together, communication is how we get the job done as a team or organization. Imagine a sports team who cannot huddle, call plays, or signal to one another during competition; that would hardly be a "team" at all. In the workplace, activity coordination communication is all about those streams of messages in constant movement back and forth that move us forward together. Work-talk, emails, brainstorming sessions, directive-giving and receiving, meetings, and collaboration are forms of this fundamental flow.

For entrepreneurs, activity coordination is about getting others to work together to produce a good or service well. When processes do not yet exist and there is little or no experience with making the new good or providing the new service, activity coordination communication fires up and gets going. We answer for each other questions about the micro, work-related issues of who does what, when, and how within these conversations. Activity coordination communication early in a new business will also often rely on discussing past experiences or the patterns we can observe from the competition so that they can be adopted, adapted, or mimicked.

Membership negotiation. Membership negotiation refers to meaning-making involved with socializing individuals into members (and back again), such as hiring, onboarding, renewal rituals, and terminations. Membership negotiation has to do with the high stakes of attracting potential members and making them into full-fledged and contributing members. Additionally, membership negotiation involves the opposite direction: figuring out when members are not contributing and dissolving that membership. Recruiting conversations, employment interviews, hiring and contract negotiations, early employment training sessions, annual awards ceremonies, employment evaluations and annual reviews, development opportunities and remediation, probationary warnings and contracts, and terminations are forms of this fundamental flow.

For entrepreneurs, membership negotiation is all about getting together a strong team of early members who have diverse knowledge and skills to meet the challenge of providing the new good or service. The newness of a new organization tends to mean that creativity and initiative are helpful qualities in the first members. Those first members will need to help create (through *their* communication) much of the organization. Thus, the entrepreneur will have to communicate to attract, select, and retain significant talent; failure to communicate successfully in attracting qualified members can mean organizational constitution cannot take shape or will dissolve soon thereafter. Additionally, getting those early members to attract, select, and retain still more quality members means that membership negotiation communication remains important and its responsibilities are passed forward to other communicators in a distributed fashion. Likewise, firing those members who are a detriment to organizational constitution quickly and professionally is essential for the entrepreneur and early team (see Chapter 4).

Self-structuring. Self-structuring refers to meaning-making involving division of labor responsibilities and role expectations. Self-structuring is all about prescribing the kinds of boss-employee, teammate, and coworker-coworker relationships that you find in organizations. This communication type gives a sense of predictability to the flow of accountability, evaluation, and assigning rewards. When an organizational chart gets created or rearranged, self-structuring communication produced it. Knowing who is responsible for what tasks and who will be responsible for evaluating those tasks is helpful in operating a team, division, unit, or organization. Much of our notions of authority, power, and politics in the workplace shape and are shaped by this type of communication. Self-structuring communication is all about the social arrangements that make *workplace* relationships distinct from other kinds of relationships.

Entrepreneurs must engage in self-structuring communication to divide labor and responsibilities; otherwise, no clear sense of direction and leadership are possible. Early members will want to know what the expectations are for their role and who reports to whom. Bitterness and confusions can tear apart workplaces if co-workers misunderstand their power relationships. A proactive, fair, and transparent approach to establishing rights and privileges is needed. As an organization grows, more members and resources will be added; therefore, self-structuring conversations will have to be engaged with and accomplished again and again.

Institutional positioning. Institutional positioning refers to meaning-making involved with presenting the organization *as an* organization. Institutional positioning is all about those messages that project the organization's image to stakeholders. Think here about advertising, marketing, branding, regulatory adaptation, political activism, and vendor negotiations. Discussions about uniforms, signage, company colors, slogans, letterhead, and logos are all a part of this flow. When institutional positioning communication is done well, it can earn a company widespread legitimacy in the eyes of key audiences. Here, legitimacy has a double meaning: Legitimacy means key stakeholders think the collective action is a *real*, genuine, or serious organization and it means the organization is seen as legally and *ethically* bona fide. Those intangible perceptions of legitimacy can, in turn, bring the tangible outcomes of investors' capital, vendors' credit, customers' purchases, and members' allegiances. Conversely, investors, vendors, and customers can decide a would-be founder or group of people is not a legitimate organization. A cute idea, a nice dream, or an interesting hobby is not the kinds of meanings that will move critical people and resources into and through a new organization.

For entrepreneurs, managing impressions with investors, vendors, and customers through institutional positioning communication is "chief and primordial" to establishing a new organization.[11] Investment dollars get secured through networking conversations and persuasive pitches. Entrepreneurs and early members must present the social fiction of the new organization *as* an organization. They do so through the creation of symbols, such as logos, signage, websites, and other branding attempts. The whole endeavor often hinges on the success or failure of this communication (see Chapter 5).

The confluence of flows. It is important to note that the FFM suggests that organizing (verb form) emerges from the overlap of two or more of the four flows and organization (noun form) emerges from the overlap of two or more of the four flows consistently over time and space. In keeping with the watery metaphor, organizations are, therefore, a "confluence" of many communication flows. A single flow is not enough. Interviewing a potential employee may be membership negotiation communication, but if no other flow is present, the conversation remains an isolated conversation—not an organization.

On the other hand, imagine, for example, one friend helping another friend move a piano up three flights of stairs. Tough work. The two will need some self-structuring and activity coordination ("I'll go up the stairs first walking backwards. You take the bottom.... Move a little to the right. Can you hold it higher, please?!"). In one sense, those interactions mean the friends are organizing (verb form) themselves to complete a shared task. Yet, few of us would feel comfortable labeling the friends an "organization" in the common use of that word.

Indeed, we reserve the designation of organization (noun form) for where all four flows are intermingling across time and space. In other words, perhaps the friends decide to start a small piano-moving business. In which case, they would need to create a company name and advertise their service (institutional positioning), hire more movers or decide to remain the two of them (membership negotiation), decide which one will handle customer service and which one will handle accounting functions (self-structuring), and work together to get primary and secondary work functions accomplished on a daily and weekly basis (activity coordination). Their existence as an organization will remain unsettled until they gain some success in each of these flows across time and space.

Exactly when the organization's existence gets established and settled is fuzzy and blurry. The process of being established as an organization is rarely "on or off," absent one moment and present the next. Instead, at its inception, it is more a matter of fading in and out, of gaining or losing momentum. As a quick aside, the point that the constitution of organizations can involve a liminal stage—at times, an organization can be neither completely present nor completely absent—was not clearly articulated in early CCO theorizing. However, scholars have begun to describe that important caveat because it follows logically from much of these writings. In sum, the FFM involves an expansive, holistic, and multilayered view of how communication constitutes organizations—one that is not reducible to any one task or activity.[12]

Six Premises of the FFM and Their Implications for Entrepreneurs

In the following pages, we outline six key premises upon which the FFM of CCO theory is built. These assumptions are especially helpful to consider prior to introducing the SEA model of organizational constitution. Where the FFM describes the communicative constitution of organization in broad terms, the SEA model (see Chapter 2 for details) borrows its main premises and uses them to prescribe specifically how to create and maintain new organizations, such as a new business.

Premise 1. Organizations are complex and not reducible to a single communication flow. When McPhee and Zaug proposed the FFM, they were responding to a trend in scholarly circles that they disliked—a classically-curmudgeon scholarly motivation for theorizing, isn't it? The trend which McPhee and Zaug disliked was to explain organizations as the product of a single communication dynamic. For example, some scholars were advocating that organizations emerge from within language use when two communicators oriented their interaction toward an object.[13] Still others proposed conversational and narrative-based linguistic structures to explain the communicative constitution of organizations.[14] Despite being sophisticated writings, they had in common the assumption that organization is the byproduct of a single communication mechanism, and that organizing is, for lack of a better word, *easy.*

McPhee and Zaug disagreed. They reasoned that organizations are much too complicated for any one communication type to explain how communication constitutes organizations.[9] Thus, their contribution was to identify the four flows and emphasize that multiple flows had to be present for organization to surface. This premise of the FFM may seem obvious but it holds important implications: Namely, the communicative constitution of organization is not an easy process, but a difficult one; additionally, this premise implies that the constitution of a new organization usually requires multiple partners' activities, not only those of a single individual or lone entrepreneur (see Premises #2 and #3 below). That means that entrepreneurs should recognize that founding a new organization requires attending to many activities at once, which very likely requires other partners to accomplish.

Premise 2. The communicative constitution of organization is difficult. Reflecting on the FFM helps us hold in the mind's eye how many disparate things must happen and go well for a new organization to come forth. Consider again the stark survival statistics of new businesses in the United States.[3] In fact, our cities and communities are full of organizations that *are not normal*, precisely because of their survival. Perhaps our everyday exposure to surviving organizations of all kinds tends to produce the unsubstantiated assumption that establishing an organization must therefore be easy.

Think of it this way: In World War II, Allied forces investigated where airplanes—which were returning from missions—had been shot most often. The reasoning went like this: If you could know where airplanes got shot most often, you could add stronger steel reinforcements to those parts of the airplanes and incorporate that knowledge into future airplane designs. Sounds smart, right? Not so much. Abraham Wald, a mathematician working for the American military, pointed out the tremendous flaw in the logic, one termed "survivorship bias."[15] The patterns of bullet holes were from *surviving* airplanes; yet reinforcements added to airplanes should be based on the pattern of bullet holes in airplanes that were shot down (which, of course, were rarely found intact enough to study). To be clear, this premise is not described to discourage or de-motivate would-be entrepreneurs. On the contrary, this premise is a means of celebrating the distributed and multifaceted work of founding a new organization.

Premise 3. Constitutive organizational leadership will tend to have a distributed quality. The FFM implies that one or even two individuals will probably not be able to mix all four flows themselves well enough to establish an organization, except for the most rudimentary of organizations (think, a summer-time shaved ice stand). A new company, church, or charity of any size will quickly demand that activities must be coordinated, membership needs to be negotiated, the organization's structure must be drafted and re-drafted, and the organization's image needs to be positioned and repositioned to investors, vendors, customers, clients, and members. Generally speaking, that is too many activities for one or two individuals to accomplish and accomplish well.

Without question, effective and ethical leadership is important for the performance and well-being of organizations.[16] Yet, here, we direct attention to a specific form of leadership, *constitutive* leadership—those efforts undertaken to influence the establishment and maintenance of a new organization. Constitutive leadership is all about influencing others to participate in the activities and communication flows that bring organization into being. For example, consider a scenario in which a founder delegates the responsibility of creating a marketing plan to a group of new members who have a background in marketing. One energetic member gets the group organized to brainstorm artwork (i.e., activity coordination), check print pricing, meet with a website designer, and so on (i.e., institutional positioning work). In doing so, both the founder and the de facto team leader are participating in constitutive leadership, leadership which has become "distributed" across the members.[16]

Much has been written about shared leadership and participatory decision-making. Sharing leadership refers to the practice of decentralizing power and influence across team members. Scholarship has established, for example, that shared leadership is especially helpful in the co-production of creativity-intensive work and industries.[17] Shared leadership invites more voices and activates higher cognitive engagement as individuals feel more responsible for outcomes and therefore offer greater cognitive effort.

Communication research demonstrated that ordinary communication practices, such as asking good questions and explicitly voicing permission for others to lead can initiate and support shared leadership.[17] Likewise, participatory decision-making refers to the practice of gathering and implementing employees' voices and input into big and small organizational decisions. Workplaces where participatory decision-making is a norm tend to catch risk and safety issues more reliably[18] and make more creative decisions.[19] While both shared leadership and participatory decision-making are usually great practices in established organizations, this third premise has a somewhat different emphasis. The point here is that the communication activities that constitute organizations tend to be so multifaceted that the leading of constitution means one person will rarely, if ever, be able to do it alone. The diversity of those flows makes it apparent that leading the creation of a new organization will likely require many individuals to influence others and help implement constitutive activities.

Premise 4. Internal and external communication *both* matter to survival and thriving. The FFM makes it clear that the organizational communication that counts for establishing and maintaining a new firm is both inside and outside the new organizational entity. Organizational communication scholars tend to avoid the language of "internal" and "external" communication for a variety of reasons. First, those labels tend to imply that the organization is a mere container or conduit for communication—and not constituted *by* communication. Second, those labels can keep us from seeing that employees often hear, see, and are affected by the organization's external advertising and branding; meanwhile, non-members hear about the communication of the workplace, which can affect their perceptions of an organization.[20]

Despite these drawbacks, we use the language of internal and external communication as convenient shortcuts to describe an interrelationship among constitutive entrepreneurial activities. Activity coordination and self-structuring are important internal constitutive flows. They are essential to getting work done. Meanwhile, institutional positioning is an essential external constitutive flow. Getting the attention and positive esteem of investors, vendors, clients, and customers must be done if the organization is going to get needed and ongoing infusions of resources (e.g., money). Membership negotiation seems to be somewhere in between. Membership negotiation is about managing the boundary. Making the right outsiders into the right insiders can help with the survival of a new organizational venture. To attract and recruit skilled individuals who can help with the distributed nature of constitutive leadership is itself a constitutive act. The point is neither internal nor external flows are enough. The absence or weakness of either kind of flow can mean a new organization fails before it begins.

Think, for example, of the charismatic entrepreneurs of Silicon Valley in the late 1990s. Some of these individuals were strong at institutional positioning. They managed to network with investors and shareholders, glad-handing and persuading them into believing in the brilliance of their technological visions. Some, however, could not deliver; they overpromised and underperformed as startup organizations. In other words, their external organizational communication of institutional positioning outpaced their internal organizational communication of activity coordination and self-structuring. The net result was a bubble burst. Conversely, imagine how many weekend, car-savvy mechanics have reasoned that they could "go into business for themselves" without giving any thought or effort to obtaining investors, vendors, or customers through branding, marketing, and advertising. The consequence is a painfully lonely decline as the mechanic waits in a hot garage for others to take notice.

Premise 5. Change can happen quickly, but it often doesn't. The FFM directs our attention to where the action is: Namely, in both people's actions as well as the structures they create and recreate with those actions. As described above, the FFM derives its inspiration from structuration theory. The theory explains that changes in social structures (such as organizations) can happen quickly but often occur slowly and incrementally, if at all. The idea is that, on one hand, organizations are human creations and so they are subject to change by humans at any moment. On the other hand, *past* human actions tend to enable and constrain all *present* human actions and so big changes will tend to be rather rare. Thus, the FFM is all about, well, *flow.* Flows move over time and space. What started upstream will greatly influence what happens downstream.

Considered from the framework of another metaphor, the communicative constitution of organization involves *momentum* and *inertia.* Momentum refers to the reality that resting objects tend to stay resting and moving objects tend to stay moving. Inertia is the idea that resting or moving objects *resist* changes in direction. When no organization yet exists, that "resting" state can be said to resist existence. Meanwhile, when a large organization gets going with a lot of members, history, and resources, it can be difficult to change directions, becoming too big to stop or change. Thus, entrepreneurs and early members seeking to create a new organization must grapple with this initial inertial resistance and seek to generate constitutive momentum.

This reasoning leads us to consider how new entrepreneurial ventures must overcome the problem of not having many social patterns or material resources flowing to it from upstream.

Premise 6. Only some, not all, communication is constitutive. An important implication of the FFM is that only some kinds of communication are constitutive of organization.[9] Of course, we communicate for all kinds of reasons that do not necessarily involve initiating or sustaining organizations—apologizing, begging, chiding, deriding, echoing, feigning interest, and grandstanding, just to name a few. The FFM suggests that it is not so much about the quantity of communication that makes organizations what they are, but the specific quality of that communication. Thus far, we explained the four specific kinds of communication flows that, when overlapping and intermingling across time and space, come to make organizations what they are. Yet, remember that a whole world of communication possibilities exists outside of those flows, which are *not* constitutive of organizations.

That premise is helpful within the context of initiating and maintaining a new organization because it is a reminder that communication is by no means a panacea or positive. "Mere talk leads only to poverty" is the way King Solomon explained it (NIV; Proverbs 14:23). Communication, conversing, and chatting is a fun pastime with family and friends; however, *mere* talk is not helpful for establishing and maintaining a new organization. The *right* communication and resources are needed.

Three Addendums about Material Resources (aka What about Money?)

Despite achieving widespread acceptance in scholarly circles in communication,[2] CCO theory in general, and the FFM in particular, had a problem. Perhaps you found yourself asking about material resources, such as money, equipment, and facilities. Everyone knows that forming a new company, charity, or church requires resources. Obtaining resources is often seen as the biggest barrier to the establishment of a new organization. In other words, doesn't matter, matter?[21]

CCO theorists acknowledged that early versions of these theories could be excessively focused on issues related to the social construction of organizations. In short, social construction is the idea that shared meanings among people create a significant portion of our lived experiences of reality.[14] Fortunately, later revisions addressed the question of material resources directly. The following three points are addendums to the FFM, which help to make it clear where and how material resources fit. The six premises above and these three material-related addendums are important because they form the conceptual foundation of the prescriptive SEA model, which we describe in the following chapter.

Addendum 1. All communication is, at least partially, material. Before discussing the role of materials in the FFM, it is important to realize that materials are not the opposite of communication.[22] All communication has an element that is physical, auditory, written, or visual. In other words, all signs, symbols, or messages have a material element. Logos, company colors, and signage are symbols and words with a very material element to them. In this way, without mentioning it directly, the four flows point us to materials.

Materials are baked into the cake, as it were. Activity coordination could involve emails, text messages, or nonverbal cues that can be recorded or observed. Self-structuring communication might involve formal meetings, employee handbooks, and organization charts that can be recorded, copied, or forwarded. Membership negotiation might involve recruitment materials, interview guides, onboarding videos, annual evaluation forms, and payroll software. Institutional positioning might involve promotional materials, business cards, letterhead, signs, logos, mailers, websites, podcasts, and video commercials. The four constitutive flows will always have a material element because all communication is, at least partially, material. Therefore, the production of these kinds of signs, symbols, and messages becomes a part of the "materializing"[21] of a new organization from nothing to something.

Addendum 2. Material resources can enable and constrain members' ability to enact any of the four flows (aka unequal constitutive capacity). The ability to enact each of the four flows can be eased through material resources, while a lack of material resources can hamstring the successful uptake of flows.[22] Getting investors, vendors, customers, and even members to perceive a new venture as a legitimate organization is difficult. However, significant reserves of money to purchase facilities, signage, employees, and equipment make obtaining those perceptions much easier.[23]

Even in an age of virtual communication and cyberspace, physical spaces and expensive artifacts (e.g., desks, conference tables, and machinery) just signal better than a lot of talk that a legitimate organization has arrived or is to be assumed. Stuff matters. Of course, material resources, such as physical spaces and expensive artifacts, do not, in themselves, make organizations what they are. A beautiful, but empty, office space can be professionally staged for potential renters—none of whom would stroll around the hallways imagining that they are experiencing an organization. No, it takes people and people communicating for that perception and reality to arise.

Nonetheless, everyone knows talk is cheap and conference tables are pricey. Interacting with others around a well-appointed conference table in a professional-looking building signals strongly to members and non-members alike that organization is present and happening. These observations suggest that material resources can help members enact the flows; meanwhile, a lack of material resources can hinder members' ability to enact the flows. This reality is summed up in the phrase, *unequal constitutive capacity*. In other words, not all are equally capable of engaging with and mixing the constitutive communication flows, and the ability to leverage material resources is a main determining factor. The unequal constitutive capacity addendum helps us see that materials facilitate constitution and make managing perceptions easier. In other words, materials can be about credibility.

Activity coordination can be easier with expensive smartphones. Attracting and hiring new members is just easier if making payroll is not a problem (i.e., membership negotiation). Getting key stakeholders to perceive a new business venture as a legitimate organization is just easier with physical space, nice furnishings, professional signage, branding, and advertisement (i.e., institutional positioning). Unequal constitutive capacity is a reality, and often it is a very unfortunate reality. Sexism, racism, structural inequalities, the exploitation of poor nations by wealthy nations (and so many other social ills) are each important reasons why this second addendum to the four flows matters and must be taken seriously in a well-rounded discussion of how organizations are constituted—or fail to be constituted.

Given Dee's experiences as a woman entrepreneur, we will be touching on the challenges presented by sexism in founding an organization as well as the benefits afforded to her company by governmental remediation efforts as a woman business owner in the US. We call for future scholarship to continue to explore and explain the many ways this second addendum plays out and its implications for diversity and inclusion in the constitution of new organizations. Being clear about how material resources can enable and constrain constitutive capacity is helpful in describing reality accurately before we move to articulating our prescriptive model for the constitution of a new organization.

· **Addendum 3. Material resources can be given organizational meanings through communication (aka materials-as-symbols).** The first two addendums direct our attention to the idea that constitutive flows always have a material quality and ample material resources can make enacting constitutive flows easier. The third addendum directs our attention to the idea that some constitutive communication in organizations is about making *materials into symbols* that represent the organization.[22] In other words, some materials get created and communicated in such a way as to become communication shortcuts for the meaning of the organization.

Consider how much communication occurs in organizations that are designed to produce artifacts that remind members and non-members alike that an organization exists and should be taken seriously. Obsessive discussions about business cards, logos, and branding are obvious examples. Logos and colors that will go on t-shirts, signs, delivery trucks, advertisements, websites, mugs, pens, and hats are all a part of members attributing an organizational meaning to material resources. In large organizations, the architecture of buildings and whole campuses can become a matter of materializing the organization and proving its legitimacy to all. Indeed, architecture is argument. In sum, all these materials get imbued with a meaning that says, "Look! All this stuff proves that we are a legitimate organization."

This is no small point. Each of the three addendums reminds us that communication and materials are not opposites. There might be a temptation to think in contrasting terms, such as communication or material, symbolic or monetary, fuzzy chitchat, or real business dealings. This book, and the SEA model in particular, seek to avoid these false dichotomies and recognize that *both* communication *and* materials matter and they are not mere opposites. Communication and materials are partial synonyms (Addendum #1), they interact to boost or damage perceptions of credibility (Addendum #2), and they can influence one another reciprocally (Addendum #3).

Entrepreneur versus Entrepreneurial

Thus far, we used the term "entrepreneur" frequently. In the remaining chapters of the book, we tend to use the term "entrepreneurial" and "entrepreneurial activities" more often. The vocabulary shift is an intentional one. Formally, an entrepreneur is a person who undertakes financial risks of starting a new business venture. By that definition, Dee is, indeed, an entrepreneur. She started a printing company and needed to risk a lot of money to do so. Twenty-five years later, she sold the business for a substantial profit.

The word entrepreneur derives from the French building blocks, *entre*, meaning "between" and *prendre*, meaning "to take." The first usage of the modern version of the word dates to 1680 and seems to direct attention to the person who *takes* the financial risk *in between* source suppliers and end-point customers.[24] In other words, taking on financial risk and being situated in a chain of production and consumption are distinctives to entrepreneurship.

Thus, the word, entrepreneur is, in one sense, an identity label. An entrepreneur is a person. That label, however, may narrow the focus by subtly getting us to study persons—their creativity, personality, or intellect—while missing a larger story of how communication makes organizations, including new businesses, what they are. To be clear, we do not mean to create a false dichotomy. Individuals can indeed have psychological dispositions, such as risk tolerance,[25] that make them more likely to become entrepreneurs. On the other hand, those individuals will need to communicate with others to establish and maintain an organization where one did not previously exist.

The reader will note that we tend to use the adjectival phrase, *entrepreneurial activities*, to put the focus on those actions (plural) that are taken by many people during the establishment and maintenance of a new organization, which include actions taken by entrepreneurs, but is not limited to them exclusively. For us, using the word entrepreneurial is a means of directing attention to the intentions or consequences of activities that create and maintain a new organization rather than the psychology of individuals. Furthermore, we use the term activities to direct attention to actions, relating, tasks, deliberations, and efforts, that is, the *doing* of things. The noun entrepreneur is about being; entrepreneurial activities are about doing—doing that can be done by anyone, not only those who are risking finances but certainly including them as well.

To be sure, we are not alone in expanding the use of terms, such as entrepreneur and entrepreneurial. Modern entrepreneurship studies are keen to include investigations of *entrepreneurial mindsets* (i.e., innovativeness exhibited by any member of an established organization), *social* entrepreneurship (i.e., solving social problems through new and innovative organization creation) and *corporate* entrepreneurship (i.e., developing new products and services from within established firm). These many cognate cousins of the term entrepreneur within the entrepreneurship literature indicate intellectual curiosity, open-mindedness, and willingness to explore new possibilities—very appropriate, don't you think?

Yet another issue with the noun, entrepreneur, involves some of the unfortunate mental baggage that comes along with it. Research suggests that for many people the label entrepreneur tends to be associated with mental images of technology and male-ness,[26] which, is, of course, as wrong as it is problematic. The myth of the (assumed male) 20-year-old college dropout tech whiz-kid entrepreneur looms large in popular imagination.[27] However, that mental image is inaccurate and has the consequence of making some (female) entrepreneurs reluctant to label themselves in these terms.

Data suggest that most entrepreneurs are neither young, nor college dropouts, nor majored in science, technology, engineering, or mathematics (STEM) fields.[27] As we observe the fabric of local businesses around our own cities, we can easily see that *most* of them are not directly involved with providing a techy good or service. Although, we are certainly glad that many do!

Admittedly, the majority of U.S.-based entrepreneurs are male. As of 2018, women-owned firms accounted for only 19.9% of all firms with employees; however, that percentage seems to be rising slowly.[28] The widespread stereotype of the male entrepreneur may be subtly reinforced in our everyday talk and stories about entrepreneurs. In media portrayals, entrepreneurs are often male and masculine to the extent that the mental image of a male entrepreneur becomes normalized in our shared taken-for-grantedness.[26]

However, that stereotype can be very problematic for women. The assumed maleness of the label, entrepreneur, may keep women from choosing this career path, or even keep them from describing themselves with the term despite being one definitionally. In fact, in early discussions between Ryan and Dee about co-authoring this book, Dee—despite her extensive experience as an entrepreneur—was a little reluctant to use the label, preferring the title "business founder and owner" (which she was as well). Upon further reflection, we realized that she found the mental image of an entrepreneur to diverge too much from her female and non-techy self-concept. Such is the power of portrayals, stereotypes, and implicit associations for understanding ourselves. We return to discussing the implications of Dee's experiences as a female entrepreneur in later chapters.

Organizational Communication and Entrepreneurship Literatures

Given the widespread acceptance of these ideas in the modern field of communication, it may surprise you to learn that precious little has been written about how the FFM describes, predicts, or explains new entrepreneurial organizational enterprises. The FFM is all about explaining the kinds of communication that calls organization into being. Seems like a good fit to explore entrepreneurship, right? We agree but that has not happened much until now.[29]

We are quick to point out that some important CCO work has described how communication co-constructs the identity of entrepreneur and entrepreneurial cultures (think, Silicon Valley),[30] but little, if any, work from the FFM focuses directly on "the communicative practices associated with ventures'—especially nascent organizations'—efforts to become viable and established firms."[30] We find that odd, given the model's main focus on how organizing and organization emerge from within communication. That lack of scholarship, however, provides us with a great opportunity to contribute to the FFM literature a focus on entrepreneurship and to invite entrepreneurship scholars to explore what CCO theory can offer.

You may be asking, if the FFM has not been used for explaining entrepreneurship, what has it been used for? The answer may surprise you. To date, four flows scholarship has been used productively to investigate when and how organizations decline or dissolve. In other words, to date, four flows scholarship has been focused on the end of organizations' lifecycles and not on their beginning.

Four flows and the decline of organizations. At the turn of the 21st century, terrorism and combatting terrorist organizations were top of mind. World-changing terrorist attacks, such as the 9/11 attacks, had media outlets and their pundits proclaiming that Islamist terror organizations were unlike any organization we have ever seen. Supposedly, these new organizations were made up of autonomous teams (i.e., sleeper cells) that required little or no direction to coordinate attacks—they were a network of terror with no structure or head. Anxieties about the looming threat to national security motivated some organizational communication scholars to consider whether the principles outlined in CCO theory could be applied to accelerating the decline of these clandestine terrorist organizations.[31] In other words, could the four flows teach us tactical lessons about how to combat—not just individual terrorists—but the terrorist *organizations* that support and direct terrorists?

For example, organizational communication scholars took on the task of analyzing 17 Abbottabad documents.[31] The Abbottabad documents are a collection of al-Qa'ida's internal organizational communiqués. The documents were captured by U.S. Navy special forces members during the raid on Osama Bin Laden's compound on May 2, 2011. The translated and publicly available documents make it apparent that Bin Laden, the al-Qa'ida leader, was attempting to keep his hidden terrorist organization operational, despite extreme disruptions from U.S. and allied forces.

The Abbottabad documents revealed a surprise of organizational curiosity: Despite the conjectures that hidden terrorist organizations were unlike any organization known to date, the documents reveal a much more mundane realization. The documents "clearly show that Bin Laden and other al-Qa'ida leaders sought... [to create

ordinary matters of] centralization, increased hierarchical ordering, and tighter coordination."[32] The documents are interesting
precisely because they are so ordinary. They reveal an organization
coming apart at the seams because of challenges to successful communication in membership negotiation, institutional positioning,
activity coordination, and self-structuring imposed by al-Qa'ida's
enemy's military operations. Taken together, the Abbottabad documents represent powerful evidence of the truth of CCO theory and
the FFM in particular.

In another four flows analysis of organizational decline, scholars
used the model to explain how a nonprofit organization became
chronically abusive to its employees.[33] The tragic case study was
conducted in a community women's center, which was founded to
help battered women escape domestic violence. As the story goes,
after 11 years of faithful service, the women's center's first director
needed to step down from leadership. The women's center was low
on funding and located in a rural area, making it difficult to attract
new and talented management. Eventually, one of the women's center counselors, Sue, accepted the job and its small paycheck, despite
having no management experience or training.

Sue bullied, humiliated, and verbally abused employees. She
threatened and screamed. When some employees went to the board
of directors to sound the alarm, they were met with a passive and
hands-off response from the board. Sue worked to consolidate her
power and the board passively acquiesced. She fired employees and
made it more difficult for the remaining employees to speak to the
board of directors at all, much less about her behavior. In response,
hiring managers focused their attention on hiring "thick-skinned"
employees and prepared them to expect abusive supervision. Of
course, these experiences were talked about throughout the local
grapevine of the rural town; eventually, it was difficult to attract
new hires at all. The women's center's reputation tanked. The weak
board did not react out of fear of a wrongful termination lawsuit
from Sue. Years passed and the nonprofit organization declined,
ethically and operationally.

The case, while heartbreaking, is powerful in that it illustrates
how the organization's decline is not merely the result of one person's actions. While Sue was certainly a "bad apple" of a leader,
her actions were amplified by a "bad barrel" of an organization in
that the abuse was either left unchecked or even promoted throughout the organization's constitutive flows. The organization itself
was abusive and declined because its constitutive flows became

corrupted. The promotion of Sue and the laissez-faire board of directors were problematic forms of self-structuring communication; membership negotiation communication included implicit warnings of abuse and focused on hiring employees who could endure abuse; and daily threats from management spread to coworker-coworker conversations setting a terrible tone and tenor for activity coordination communication. No wonder the organization itself declined. Taken together, these research examples demonstrate that the FFM has strong explanatory power for specifying how and why organizations decline, dissolve, or disintegrate. While those insights are powerful, they leave us wanting to know more about the other side of the coin: the establishment and maintenance of healthy organizations.

Thus, currently, the CCO scholarship is in a curious state of play. These ideas have been used more often to understand the decline of organizations than to understand their establishment and maintenance. We contribute to the CCO theory literature and the FFM in particular a focus on entrepreneurial activities as well as a prescriptive extension of the descriptive model. Our hope is that this book stimulates more scholarship into the interplay between entrepreneurship (of all kinds) and CCO theorizing.

Insights from the entrepreneurship literature. Without question, the entrepreneurship literature is expansive, and this book certainly does not attempt to summarize it. Others have done that work and done it much better than we could.[34] Our aim, however, is to stimulate crosstalk between the communication and entrepreneurship literatures. This book is about explaining how communication makes new organizations what they are, calling them into being and sustaining them (or not). In doing so, we attend to the activities between and among many individuals that account for the birth of new organizations. That focus complements many of the sophisticated insights already known from the field of entrepreneurship, but it also contributes a new way of thinking about and researching entrepreneurship as a communication phenomenon.

Much is known about the psychological dispositions, cultures, and incentives that account for those who tend to become an entrepreneur. For example, research indicated that entrepreneurs tend to have a high need for achievement and a high tolerance for ambiguity.[34,35] Need for achievement refers to a longing for substantial accomplishments such that an individual will demonstrate significant self-denial, determination, and effort in the pursuit of long-term goals. Makes sense, doesn't it? Starting a new business takes drive and a lot of hard work now for the possibility of reward later. A review of more than 40 studies confirmed that the need for achievement is significantly associated with individuals' selection of entrepreneurship as a career as well as the performance of the firms that those entrepreneurs establish.[35]

Similarly, and perhaps unsurprisingly, entrepreneurship studies document that individuals with high tolerance for ambiguity are more likely to become entrepreneurs. Of course, entrepreneurs must cope with a great deal of ambiguity in the marketplace and uncertainties associated with what to do next. Research indicated that entrepreneurs tend to view ambiguous data more positively than managers and even report less stress associated with role ambiguities (having vague and changing job demands) as compared to blue or white-collar workers.[35] Such lists of traits paint an interesting picture of who tends to choose the occupation of entrepreneur; however, trait-based theories are fading in popularity. For the most part, entrepreneurship scholars moved away from trait-based studies of entrepreneurs.

Entrepreneurship scholars worry that trait-based theories can distort our view of entrepreneurship by overvaluing the role played by personality.[35] Additionally, and less obviously, trait theories of entrepreneurship may inadvertently imply that entrepreneurship is an innate attribute, rather than one which can be learned, grown, and even incentivized by social and economic environments. In other words, a problematic "born not bred" mentality can be implied by these studies, which modern entrepreneurship studies want to avoid.[36] Two entrepreneurship scholars described it this way:

While personality trait approach is intuitively appealing, personality theories do not adequately explain why some individuals engage in entrepreneurial behavior and others do not. Indeed, studies focusing on entrepreneurs' personality traits have been widely criticized, and have fallen out of favor ... most entrepreneurs do not possess all the [known] ideal positive traits. Further, people who are not entrepreneurs can possess several ideal personality traits.[37]

Another potential drawback of attending too exclusively to trait approaches is that they may obscure the essential role played by many communication *partners* in the establishment of a new business. Communication between and among new members and external stakeholders will come to form the being of any new organization created. In this way, not only the psyche of one individual matters. Of course, entrepreneurs' personality shapes the kinds of conversations and listening that occur, but focusing too exclusively on personality could lead us to miss the forest for the trees, to miss the whole because of an obsession with the part.

In addition to personality theories, entrepreneurship research has explored larger governmental and societal forces that present barriers or facilitators to entrepreneurial ventures and new firm creation. One study of 82 countries—ranging from Albania to Zimbabwe—demonstrated empirically that new firms are more plentiful in countries where it is easier to start a business and where there is less political corruption.[38] Comparably light regulations and little bureaucratic red tape help new businesses get going. Similarly, where entrepreneurs have confidence that they can enjoy the fruits of their efforts fairly—without government authorities picking their pockets—the launching of new businesses is much more likely. Such insights are extremely relevant and help us think about entrepreneurial activities as situated within much larger social structures that facilitate or interfere with the creation of new business organizations. Alas, few of us have much control over whether our nation of origin can streamline regulations associated with starting a new business or whether political corruption is common.

In addition to social and governmental forces, entrepreneurship research documented the obvious and significant role played by money in determining who becomes an entrepreneur. Starting a new service-based organization or manufacturing firm requires a lot of upfront expense. That means money will have a big influence on who starts a new business. Interestingly, research demonstrated a relationship between whether an individual has received a large gift or inheritance and the likelihood of starting a new business. The presence of even a relatively modest inheritance (roughly US $24,000.00) *doubled* the likelihood that an adult child would be a self-employed entrepreneur.[39] As the size of the inheritance grows, so too does that likelihood. Those findings are important, given that entrepreneurs and would-be entrepreneurs tend to identify a lack of capital as a main and key problem to be overcome. In other words, money matters, to say otherwise is naïve.

However, that is not to suggest that founding a business is impossible for low-wealth individuals and families. It is to suggest that "very wealthy households are more likely to start a business."[40] Again, that point makes sense, because members of wealthy households do not necessarily need to convince investors, and, if they do want investors, wealthy households tend to be a part of the same social and professional networks as other wealthy households, making it easier to find venture capital. Also, having substantial wealth reduces the perceived stakes a failed venture might have on one's quality of life. In sum, material and capital resources make the probability of entrepreneurship much more likely.

Clearly, the entrepreneurship literature offers many intriguing insights into *who*, *where*, and *when* new firms are most likely to be created. These antecedents or inputs of entrepreneurship are fascinating. This book is less about inputs of entrepreneurship and much more about the throughput of new organizational creation. We focus here on the *what* and *how* of new firms. What is an organization and how is it created and maintained? We certainly acknowledge that entrepreneurship (broadly defined) is possible without the creation of a new organization. However, our focus involves explaining those larger entrepreneurial enterprises that involve the origination of organizations in which people's efforts must be coordinated toward the implementation of value propositions.

Conclusion

In this chapter, we explained the history and basic ideas surrounding CCO theory. Then, the FFM —one of the three main traditions of CCO—was explained in detail. Six basic premises of the FFM were discussed. Then, three addendums to the FFM were explained, which make the role played by materials in the communicative constitution of organization more plain. We concluded by reviewing popular uses of the FFM to describe the decline of organizations and called for the FFM to be used in studies of new firm creation and maintenance. Finally, we situated our theorizing of entrepreneurship within the organizational communication literature; we call for greater engagement with and crosstalk between communication and entrepreneurship. No doubt, both fields have much to gain from one another. The next chapter outlines the details of the SEA model, which is a prescriptive extension of the FFM of CCO theory.

Notes

1 Gottman, J. M. (2014). *Principia amoris: The new science of love.* New York: Routledge.
2 Boivin, G., Brummans, B. H., & Barker, J. R. (2017). The institutionalization of CCO scholarship: Trends from 2000 to 2015. *Management Communication Quarterly, 31*(3), 331–355. doi:10.1177/0893318916873996.

3 U.S. Bureau of Labor Statistics (2020). Survival of private sector establishments by opening year. Retrieved from https://www.bls.gov/bdm/us_age_naics_00_table7.txt.

4 Putnam, L. L., & Nicotera, A. M. (Eds.) (2009). *Building theories of organization: The constitutive role of communication.* New York: Routledge.

5 Ferris, R. (2020, August 17). Why Hertz landed in bankruptcy court when its rivals didn't. *CNBC.* Retrieved from https://www.cnbc.com/2020/08/17/why-hertz-landed-in-bankruptcy-court-when-its-rivals-didnt.html.

6 Weick, K. E. (1979). *The social psychology of organizing* (2nd ed.). New York: McGraw Hill.

7 Daft, R. L., & Weick, K. E. (1984). Toward a model of organizations as interpretation systems. *Academy of Management Review, 9*(2), 284–295.

8 Taylor, J. R., & Van Every, E. J. (1999). *The emergent organization: Communication as its site and surface.* New York: Routledge.

9 McPhee, R. D., & Zaug, P. (2000). The communicative constitution of organizations: A framework for explanation. *Electronic Journal of Communication, 10*(1 and 2), 1–16.

10 Giddens, A. (1984). *The constitution of society.* Oakland, CA: University of California Press.

11 See p. 83 in McPhee, R. D., & Iverson, J. (2009). Agents of constitution in the communidad: Constitutive processes of communication in organizations. In L. L. Putnam, & A. M. Nicotera (Eds.), *Building theories of organization: The constitutive role of communication* (pp. 49–88). New York: Routledge.

12 Iverson, J. O., McPhee, R. D., & Spaulding, C. W. (2018). Being able to act otherwise: The role of agency in the FF at 2-1-1 and beyond. In B. H. J. M. Brummans (Ed.), *The agency of organizing: Perspectives and case studies* (pp. 43–65). New York: Routledge.

13 Newcomb, T. M. (1953). An approach to the study of communicative acts. *Psychological Review, 60*(6), 393.

14 Bisel, R. S. (2010). A communicative ontology of organization? A description, history, and critique of CCO theories for organization science. *Management Communication Quarterly, 24*(1), 124–131. doi:10.1177/0893318909351582.

15 Miller, B. (2020, August 28). How 'survivorship bias' can cause you to make mistakes. *BBC.* Retrieved from https://www.bbc.com/worklife/article/20200827-how-survivorship-bias-can-cause-you-to-make-mistakes.

16 Bisel, R. S., Fairhurst, G. T., & Sheep, M. L. (2022). CCO theory and leadership. In J. Basque, N. Bencherki, & T. Kuhn (Eds.), *Routledge handbook of CCO* (pp. 297–309). New York: Routledge.

17 Kramer, M. W. (2006). Shared leadership in a community theater group: Filling the leadership role. *Journal of Applied Communication Research, 34*(2), 141–162. doi:10.1080/00909880600574039.

18 Novak, J. M., & Sellnow, T. L. (2009). Reducing organizational risk through participatory communication. *Journal of Applied Communication Research, 37*(4), 349–373. doi:10.1080/00909880903233168.

19 Carmeli, A., Sheaffer, Z., & Halevi, M. Y. (2009). Does participatory decision-making in top management teams enhance decision effectiveness and firm performance? *Personnel Review, 38*, 696–714. doi:10.1108/00483480910992283.
20 Cheney, G., & Christensen, L. T. (2001). Organizational identity: Linkages between internal and external communication. In F. M. Jablin, & L. L. Putnam (Eds.), *The new handbook of organizational communication: Advances in theory, research, and methods* (pp. 231–269). Thousand Oaks, CA: Sage.
21 Ashcraft, K. L., Kuhn, T. R., & Cooren, F. (2009). Constitutional amendments: "Materializing" organizational communication. *Academy of Management Annals, 3*, 1–64. doi:10.5465/19416520903047186.
22 Bruscella, J. S., & Bisel, R. S. (2018). Four Flows theory and materiality: ISIL's use of material resources in its communicative constitution. *Communication Monographs, 85*(3), 331–356. doi:10.1080/03637751.2017.1420907.
23 Iverson, J. O., McPhee, R. D., & Spaulding, C. W. (2018). Being able to act otherwise: The role of agency in the FF at 2-1-1 and beyond. In B. H. J. M. Brummans (Ed.), *The agency of organizing: Perspectives and case studies* (pp. 43–65). New York: Routledge.
24 Bolton, B., & Thompson, J. (2004). *Entrepreneurs: Talent, temperament, technique* (2nd ed.). Amsterdam: Elsevier.
25 Hvide, H. K., & Panos, G. A. (2014). Risk tolerance and entrepreneurship. *Journal of Financial Economics, 111*, 200–223. doi:10.1016/j.jfineco.2013.06.001.
26 Ahl, H., & Marlow, S. (2012). Exploring the dynamics of gender, feminism and entrepreneurship: Advancing debate to escape a dead end? *Organization, 19*(5), 543–562. doi:10.1177/1350508412448695.
27 Goodwin, M. (2015, January 9). The myth of the tech whiz who quits college to start a company. *Harvard Business Review.* Retrieved from https://hbr.org/2015/01/the-myth-of-the-tech-whiz-who-quits-college-to-start-a-company.
28 Hait, A. W. (2021, March 29). Women business ownership in America on the rise: Number of women-owned employer firms increased 0.6% from 2017 to 2018. *United States Census Bureau.* Retrieved from https://www.census.gov/library/stories/2021/03/women-business-ownership-in-america-on-rise.html.
29 Koschmann, M. A. (2011). Developing a communicative theory of the nonprofit. *Management Communication Quarterly, 26*, 139–146. doi:10.1177/0893318911423640.
30 See page 96 in Kuhn, T. & Marshall, D. (2019). The communicative constitution of entrepreneurship. In J. J. Reuer, S. F. Matusik, & J. Jones (Eds.), *The Oxford handbook of entrepreneurship and collaboration* (pp. 83–113). Oxford: Oxford University Press.
31 Stohl, C., & Stohl, M. (2011). Secret agencies: The communicative constitution of a clandestine organization. *Organization Studies, 32*(9), 1197–1215. doi:10.1177/0170840611410839.
32 See page 534 in Bean, H., & Buikema, R. J. (2015). Deconstituting al-Qa'ida: CCO theory and the decline and dissolution of hidden organization. *Management Communication Quarterly, 29*, 512–538. doi:10.1177/0893318915597300.

33 Lutgen-Sandvik, P., & McDermott, V. (2008). The constitution of employee-abusive organizations: A communication flows theory. *Communication Theory, 18*(2), 304–333. doi:10.1111/j.1468-2885.2008.00324.x.
34 Casson, M., Yeung, B., & Basu, A. (Eds.) (2008). *The Oxford handbook of entrepreneurship.* Oxford: Oxford University Press.
35 Chell, E. (2008). *The entrepreneurial personality: A social construction* (2nd ed.). New York: Routledge.
36 Ginsberg, A., & Buchholtz, A. (1989). Are entrepreneurs a breed apart? A look at the evidence. *Journal of General Management, 15*(2), 32–40. doi:10.1177/030630708901500203.
37 See page 84 in Westhead, P., & Wright, M. (2013). *Entrepreneurship: A very short introduction.* Oxford: Oxford University Press.
38 Klapper, L., Amit, R., & Guillén, M. F. (2010). Entrepreneurship and firm formation across countries. In J. Lerner, & A. Schoar (Eds.), *International differences in entrepreneurship* (pp. 129–158). Chicago, IL: University of Chicago Press.
39 Blanchflower, D. G., & Oswald, A. J. (1998). What makes an entrepreneur? *Journal of Labor Economics, 16,* 26–60.
40 See page 321 in Hurst, E., & Lusardi, A. (2004). Liquidity constraints, household wealth, and entrepreneurship. *Journal of Political Economy, 112,* 319–347. doi:10.1086/381478.

2 The SEA model of New Organizational Constitution

Abstract

This chapter presents the seven entrepreneurial activities (SEA) model of new organizational constitution. The chapter opens by explaining distinctives of prescriptive theorizing and positive deviance case investigations. The SEA model suggests that when entrepreneurs' value proposition(s) are sufficiently complex to require the creation of a new organization, seven specific activities—arranged in three higher-order sets—are needed. Additionally, processes of organizational learning are described as creating constitutive momentum among those entrepreneurial activities. The subparts of the SEA model are defined and illustrated. Taken together, the SEA model contributes an original prescriptive model of new organizational constitution, which views new organizations as (a) communicative and material, (b) initiated by value proposition(s), (c) difficult to achieve, (d) having periods of partiality, (e) being the result of constitutive leadership distributed among members, and (f) dependent upon constitutive momentum generated in organizational learning.

Descriptive and Prescriptive Theory

In the social sciences, there are descriptive and prescriptive theories. A descriptive theory is a description, prediction, or explanation about what "is" the case in reality. A prescriptive theory is a description, prediction, or explanation about what "ought" to make reality better. Descriptive theory describes (like a historian or scientist); prescriptive theory prescribes (as with a medical doctor or a coach). Great descriptive theories are essential to understanding the world *as it is*. Great prescriptive theories are helpful in knowing what to do next to make our (personal) world *better* than it is. Here's the important part: Great prescriptive theories must be based on

DOI: 10.4324/9781003291312-2

great descriptive theories. Great prescriptive theories require a firm foundational picture of reality as it is. Prescriptive theory without a strong foundation of a descriptive theory spells disaster. It is the domain of wonky advice, misguided guruism, or worse.

For example, bloodletting used to be a widely prescribed medical procedure for many different ailments. The prescriptive theory is built upon the shaky descriptive theory proposed by the ancient Greek physician, Hippocrates, millennia ago. Hippocrates believed that ailments occurred when an imbalance among four bodily liquids, or humors, were present. Centuries later, a Greek physician living in Rome, Galen, used this descriptive theory in proposing his prescriptive theory that bloodletting should help the humors rebalance and combat illness.[1] Incredibly, the practice was still commonplace well into the 1800s. While both Hippocrates and Galen made very important discoveries that proved correct, these ideas certainly did not.

In a more affirmative and recent (and a little less nauseating) example, consider the social psychologist, Irving Janis's, descriptive theory of why otherwise intelligent team members can make stupid decisions when put together as a team. Janis explored various historical case studies in which brilliant political and military minds decided upon disastrous plans (think, the Bay of Pigs fiasco). Janis discovered that, in each case, brilliant individuals became slowly predisposed to agreeing with their other brilliant teammates at the collective cost of losing the ability to reflect critically; he called the resulting dynamic, *groupthink*.[2] No doubt, it is a solid descriptive theory of the (unfortunate!) reality of a lot of teamwork. In the following years, communication scholars proposed a prescriptive theory (i.e., Vigilant Interaction Theory) for combatting poor decision-making.[3] The theory recommends team members engage in three specific types[4] of conversations. Unsurprisingly, teams who follow the recommendations to discuss the negative consequences of their ideas aloud (and therefore engage in critical reflection together) are much more likely to avoid groupthink and make higher quality decisions.[3,4] In sum, if prescriptive theory stands a chance of being helpful, it must be based on a valid descriptive theory.

Yet, we must admit that even with the best foundation, prescriptive theorizing is perilous. Movement across the "is/ought" boundary means stretching from describing what reality is now to prescribing those activities that encourage reality into what we want it to be. Moving across that boundary is akin to switching from describing plant growth on paper to prescribing how to grow delicious salad ingredients in your own garden. Describing plant growth in a textbook has the advantage of working in the mind's eye, not in the dirt itself. Prescribing how to grow delicious salad ingredients involves elements that are difficult to control and account for, such as the gritty local details of external forces (rain, sun, and soil) and hard-to-quantify subjective elements (What is delicious?). Despite these challenges, practical lessons certainly exist, which differentiate the skill of the green-thumb gardener from the novice. In this same spirit, we offer the SEA model of the SEA of new organizational constitution.

By way of a preview, the SEA model is explained in this chapter. Then, in the middle of the book, Dee provides autobiographical reflections from her 25 years of entrepreneurship and business ownership to illustrate the model and to tie it more closely to lived experience—you know, to the gritty local details of organizational "gardening." Still, admittedly, models must be stated somewhat ambiguously so that they can be used in many situations. However, models can also run the risk of becoming too abstract as to render them meaningless. To avoid this possibility, our strategy is to weave together an explanation of the SEA model with autobiographical reflections of real, lived entrepreneurial experiences.

The SEA model is based on many, many conversations over the years. Dee started her company when Ryan was still in elementary school. Dee went on to sell the business after Ryan was a professor of organizational communication. Growing up, Ryan worked summers in the small shop, doing unglamorous but necessary tasks, such as cleaning toilets, removing trash, repainting walls, and making deliveries. Eventually, Ryan would learn accounting and bookkeeping functions of the company (much more glamorous, right?) and go on to use those skills in another company. Dee and Ryan's experiences as an entrepreneur/mother and (eventual) scholar/son means that our ability to articulate this model is the product of a lot of organic talking and thinking via both top-down and bottom-up processing.

Positive Deviance Case Studies

Dee's experiences as an entrepreneur were instrumental in the construction of the SEA model. For me (Ryan), Dee represents a special form of case study. Technically, Dee, and her experiences as an entrepreneur, is what is known as a case of positive deviance.[5,6] The humorous phrase, positive deviance, is a way of classifying a case for study as *un*usual—but in a *good* way. Marriages that only last a week are negative deviants; happily married couples that last 70 years are positive deviants. Criminals are negative deviants; medal of honor recipients are positive deviants. Negative deviants are disasters; positive deviants are masters. Positive deviance case studies are helpful in that they allow us to document a set of behaviors that are likely good to imitate. In other words, positive deviance case studies are a systematic way of generating recommendations and examples worthy of imitation.

Organizational scholars noticed that reports of positive deviance case studies are not as common as negative deviance case studies in academic literatures.[7] No doubt, a tremendous amount can be learned from either form of case study. Yet, scholars also argued that positive deviance case studies are especially valuable in that they can help to build a "collection of... examples worthy of... imitation."[7] There is a lot to be learned from examples of how *not* to act, but we also need examples of what to do. Think of it this way: Have you ever had a grammar teacher who could pick at your word choice, syntax, and sentence construction without ever showing you an example of a well-written essay? Sure, we need to see the errors, but we also need to see examples of what to aspire to achieve. Mastery depends upon both.

But not just any example can be considered a positive deviance case study. Fortunately, organizational scholars provided guidance on what makes for a positive deviance case. A case may be considered a positive deviant if it meets the benchmarks of (a) intentionality, (b) non-normativity, and (c) honorability. *Intentionality* refers to whether the behaviors, activities, or decisions under investigation were done on purpose. One-off happy accidents are great, but they are difficult to imitate and so there is little warrant to study those cases. We want to learn from masters, not gamblers who just got lucky once.

Non-normativity refers to the quality of being comparatively unique, rare, or unusual—in a phrase, "not normal." For social scientists, the word, normal, tends to take on a very specific and mathematical meaning that differs somewhat from its everyday use. Here, non-normativity has to do with a bell curve or normal distribution. Statistics tells us that most qualities and characteristics are normally distributed in the population such that *most* people (68.2%) vary from the average, an average amount. Read that once more: Most characteristics or qualities vary from the average, an average amount. For example, the average man in the United States stands at a height of 5 feet 10 inches. More than two-thirds of men in the United States are within a mere three inches of that height.[8]

In other words, for men in the United States, *any* height from 5 feet 7 inches to 6 feet 1 inch is "normal" comparatively and statistically speaking. Positive deviants, on the other hand, must be comparatively and statistically not normal. Non-normativity occurs when we reach well beyond ordinary boundaries of average and the average distance from that average.

A non-normative case can be "positive" to the degree that it meets the honorability criterion. In this context, *honorability* refers to those behaviors, activities, and decisions that are humane, (morally) good, noble, life-giving, wholesome, charitable, democratic, and healthy. Where non-normativity is about mathematics and statistics, honorability is about values and ideals. For example, in one study of positive deviance, the mother of a young gymnast discovered that her daughter was being verbally and physically abused by elite coaches. In response to this heartbreaking situation, the tough and enterprising mom, Alexis Reader, started her own gymnastics training facility with the purpose of finding a more humane way of training elite child-athletes than those strategies, which had become common throughout the USA Gymnastics. Her 15 years of organizational efforts resulted in a new set of strategies for training youths that presented a much-needed alternative to the harsh norm. Additionally, that humane instructional mode has already produced regional, national, and international gymnastics stars. Alexis Reader is a positive deviant because her entrepreneurial efforts are very *rare* (a deviant), and those efforts are very *noble* (positive) in correcting wrongs and doing moral good. You can read more about the incredible story of Alexis Reader's entrepreneurial activities here.[9,10]

To be clear, for us, merely making a lot of profits is not sufficient to claim honorability because profits can be made in unethical ways. For example, the utility corporation, Enron, was amazingly profitable, but, of course, it achieved large profits through nefarious means.[11] So, profitability by itself certainly does not meet the honorability criterion. Scholars have put it this way: The word, positive, in positive deviance case studies is "not meant to suggest superfluous self-help, but meaningful empirical insights about the [ethically] good life, well lived."[12]

Dee's Entrepreneurial Efforts as a Positive Deviance Case

Thus, when all three of these criteria apply to a case, a positive deviance case is established. That means that it is likely a great place to look for reliable lessons we can glean from in moving across that "is/ought boundary" between descriptive and prescriptive theory. Dee's entrepreneurial activities over the course of 25 years meet all three criteria (although, she would be much too humble to say so, if it were not for Ryan writing this part!).

First, Dee's efforts certainly meet the *intentionality* criterion. She quit a high-paying job with a multinational corporation and pursued a dream of business ownership. She invested her retirement account and a lot of sweat and tears (see Chapter 3). Yes, this endeavor was on purpose. Second, Dee's entrepreneurial successes are *non-normative* in several ways: As mentioned in the previous chapter, survival rate statistics of new small businesses indicate Dee's 25 years of being in business make her business experiences unique. U.S. Bureau of Labor statistics suggests that half of all small businesses fail before 5 years of existence and 70% of small business ventures fail within ten years.[13] These rates alone mean that Dee's small business is a survival deviant, occupying a status with less than 30% of all U.S. small businesses. Additionally, as of 2018 in the United States , women-owned firms accounted for only 19.9% of all firms with employees.[14] Furthermore, the National Association of Women Business Owners (NAWBO) estimates that 4.2% of those women-owned firms have revenues of $1 million dollars (US) or more[15]—each are benchmarks that Dee's company achieved. Thus, the longevity, women-owned status, and revenues achieved make her case one that deviates from the average.

Dee's case also meets the *honorability* criterion because of the charitable and generous approach her company took to giving to the local community (see Chapter 5, Reflection 11). Let me (Ryan) explain: *The Chronicle of Philanthropy* and American Express report that the average small U.S. firm gives 6% of company profits to charity.[16] Conservative estimates suggest that Dee's company gave 2–6 times that amount to charity every year. In fact, the company gave generously even during a few years when no annual profits were reported. Proportionately, small firms do tend to be more charitable than large corporations. Large corporations in the United States gave, on average, less than 1% of company pre-tax net income to charity.[17] In other words, Dee's company's charity standards also significantly exceeded average large corporate giving. Dee's company established a set of giving standards very early on in the company's lifecycle (see her story about charitable giving policy in the last section of the body). Dee wishes it to be known that those giving standards were inspired by the generosity she experienced as a high-ranking manager with Hallmark Cards prior to starting the company. Thus, Dee's autobiographical accounts represent a positive deviance case study ideal for developing a prescriptive theory—via historical reconstruction—of entrepreneurial activities for organizational constitution.

Brief Overview of the SEA Model

The following section outlines the major features of the SEA model. The model is based on the idea that three categories of entrepreneurial activities are needed simultaneously for a new organization to be constituted, that is, called into being. If any of the three sets of activities is missing or weakened, a new organization will be missing or so thin and partial[18] as to make its existence questionable. Organizing (verb) may be present, but organization (noun) will not. Those three categories of interrelated entrepreneurial activities include: exploring-realizing, doubting-updating, and legitimizing-multiplying/sustaining. In general, exploring-realizing involves those entrepreneurial activities that deal with discovering and implementing valued benefits for others (e.g., customers, clients) in terms of goods or services for which there is a market or for which a market can be created. Exploring-realizing are about those *second-order changes* brought about by entrepreneurial activities. They are about communicating for creatively identifying value propositions and how those ideas might be brought to bear for a market of interested others. Here, exploring-realizing entrepreneurial activities generate big, often revolutionary, second-order changes. When value propositions are sufficiently complex to require organization for implementation, then still more organizational constitution efforts are needed. In other words, exploring-realizing activities generate the first big momentum push for an organization to arise from nothing.

At the same time as exploring-realizing activities occur, organizations require doubting-updating activities in order for them to be established, survive, and thrive. Doubting-updating involves those entrepreneurial activities that deal with identifying opportunities, gaps, weaknesses, errors, mistakes, ethical lapses, ignorances, negligences, complacencies, vulnerabilities, imbalances, and inattentions and then remediating those present or potential future problems. Doubting-updating are about those *first-order* and *internal* organizational changes brought about by entrepreneurial activities. They are about communicating to seize opportunities as well as catch and fix problems—small or large—that hold back the organization from the successful delivery of valued benefits. In this way, doubting-updating deals with avoiding the incremental decaying enemy within. Despite its critical role, exploring-realizing and doubting-updating are still not sufficient to constitute a new organization.

At the same time as doubting-updating occurs, organizations also require legitimizing-multiplying/sustaining activities. Legitimizing-multiplying involves those entrepreneurial activities that deal with gaining and sustaining stakeholders' perception that an organization—not merely an individual—exists and can be trusted as a good-faith interactional and transactional partner. Legitimizing-sustaining involves avoiding those decisions that overleverage organization and undermine credibility. Legitimating-multiplying are about those *first-order* and *external* organizational changes brought about by entrepreneurial activities. They are about the numerous small and big ways the image of the organization gets communicated to the minds of stakeholders. Branding, advertising, logos, referrals, signage, and networking are just a few examples. At some point, external stakeholders begin to think of the organization in terms of these images and symbols and not in terms of one, two, or a few individuals. In doing so, stakeholders taking the organization for granted gets reflected back to members, strengthening members *and* stakeholders' perception in a reinforcing cycle. In this way, legitimizing-multiplying deals with the problem of the organization's image to be questioned in the first place or to deteriorate during interactions with stakeholders. Only when all three sets of entrepreneurial activities are enacted and succeeding will a new organization appear and be sustained sufficiently long to be thought of as an organization.

Thus, the SEA model implies that organizations are the result of the combined interactions of sub-parts, which form a new organization. Here, organization is presented as an emergent property: a whole that is irreducible to the mere sum of its parts. Emergent properties refer to those phenomena that necessarily originate from *interactions* among parts to form larger meaningful systems.

Organizational Learning: Momentum in SEA

A notable divergence between the SEA model and the four flows model involves the assumption that constitutive processes—and the activities that unfold to make organizations what they are—can

be present or absence *in degrees.* To date, most communicative constitution of organizations (CCO) theorizing assumes that organizations come into being when one or more specific communication
functions are performed. Or, to write it differently, much CCO
theorizing assumes that organization is absent when those specific communication functions are absent. Picture a toggle switch:
Organization is on or off. The theorizing portrays organization as
more of an "on or off" phenomenon than one that fades "in and
out." The SEA model, however, diverges from that assumption and
portrays new organizations gaining and losing momentum, which
means they fade in and out, usually until a tipping point is reached
in which sufficient energy, history, relationships, and materials
make them seem obvious and established. That tipping point can
be re-met on the organization's decline, such that what would seem
stable can be dissolved. In between these lifespan extremes, constitutive momentum can become so well-oiled, rapid, and smooth that
it hides from view.

But what accounts for momentum (or a failure to generate
momentum) in entrepreneurial activities that constitute new organizations?: organizational learning. Formally, organizational
learning refers to creating, disseminating, and routinizing knowledge that makes a social system more fit with its environment.[19]
Here, the word, learning, is not unlike the way children learn from
their parents how to take care of themselves more and more over
the years. As we learn, we become more fit and adapted to the
environment around us and more capable of survival and thriving
on our own.

To be clear, this idea is not new. Organizational scientists of
all stripes have pointed to learning as a key process that deter-
mines which organizations survive and thrive and which ones
fail.[19–23] Unsurprisingly, the entrepreneurship literature also uses
the learning concept increasingly. After conducting a review of
the entrepreneurship literature, one scholar commented, "It is apparent that learning is gaining acceptance as an integral element
of entrepreneurial practice and study."[24] In fact, one inductive
study of six small business owners revealed that the entrepreneurs
tended to tell the history of their respective businesses around
critical and emotionally-laden episodes of learning that the entrepreneurs recounted as important to the survival of their firms.[25]
In other words, entrepreneurs themselves point to those (often
painful) "lessons learned" that they needed to go through as crucial moments that determined their success or lack thereof. The

lessons offered by the entrepreneurial school of hard knocks appear to be more than just a saying. You will read similar stories in Chapters 3–5. In short, learning matters. The SEA model assumes that the quality of new organizations' learning is the momentum it generates or fails to generate, which is directly related to its constitutional success.

But is organizational learning communicative in nature? In other words, have we now moved away from a communicative theory of the firm? We think not. Experts of organizational learning make the case plainly with two important points about how organizational learning works. First, learning only becomes "organizational" in so far as the lessons learned are communicated to other members and teams and eventually routinized into policies or practices.[19,20] One scholar put it this way: "Any form of *organizational* learning, therefore, will require the evolution of shared mental models.... making dialogue [i.e., communication] a necessary... step in learning."[26] In other words, organizational learning requires organizational communication. Second, biased verbal conversations that employ niceties, euphemisms, and topic avoidance are some of the central culprits of organizational ignorance—or a failure of organizational learning.[22,23,27] In this way, communication is

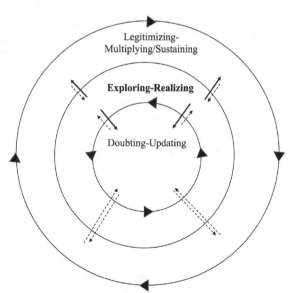

Figure 2.1 The Seven Entrepreneurial Activities (SEA) Model of New Organizational Constitution.

not merely helpful, but also can be hurtful to the organizational learning process, and therefore, in the process of constituting a new organization. More communication is not better; better is better. We might also add that the ideas of organizational learning and the communicative constitution of organizations have already been connected in communication literature, although only recently.[27] We anticipate other CCO theorists will continue to follow suit in making the connection between organizational learning and constitution more explicit.

The figure above depicts the SEA model. Organizational learning is represented by circular movements; small arrows and dotted arrows represent reciprocal interactions among activities sets. Exploring-realizing activities are bolded to connote the origin of the impetus for organization (Figure 2.1).

Exploring-Realizing: Initiating Entrepreneurial Activities

Of the three sets of activities, exploring-realizing entrepreneurial activities are most classically associated with entrepreneur as an identity label. These activities are all about those sparks of creativity or innovation that are the driving reasons for an organization's being. At its core, exploring-realizing are about both the discovery and implementation of a new firm's value proposition or value propositions. Value propositions are the desired benefit or benefits that can be provided to stakeholders, such as customers and clients. In the case of a new printing company, value propositions involve the capacity to produce custom and quality artwork and printed materials (e.g., letterhead and envelops), which other business-customers desire for their own legitimizing-multiplying activities (see below).

Exploring is all about discovering value propositions. We write, discover*ing* (verb form), to include the final discovery of value propositions but also to retain all those cognitive and communicative efforts needed to get to the final edition. Creativity is a messy process. The founders of Burger King Corporation (technically, "Insta-Burger King" at its founding) worked tirelessly to see if a new conveyor-belt machine that charbroiled burgers could give them an edge in the fast-food business. The conveyor-belt machine represents a value proposition technology, which involved the benefits of rapid time, cooking consistency, and backyard grilling taste.[28] The machine was not reliable in those early years but getting the machine into service and modifying it thereafter were essential pieces of the founders' exploring activities. Imagine the huge number of conversations—between the founders and others—to learn about the machine in the first place, decide whether it could work in their restaurant, and improve its functioning over time. Those conversations were constitutive activities. We should also mention that when it comes to entrepreneurial exploring, inspiration often takes the form of imitation and mimicry, (hopefully) with a twist. Identifying a good value proposition already established in the market and then thinking through what adjustments or tweaks are possible or desirable is a common wellspring of entrepreneurial ideas. Models are followed for a reason.

Realizing involves the implementation—or attempted implementation—of value propositions. Exploring is not enough. Implementation gets a vote. Where exploring involves creative planning and conjecture, implementation involves testing by unforgiving reality. As mentioned above, the founders of Burger King Corporation were excited about their automated, conveyor-belt burger-cooking machines. Early versions of the machine were less than impressive. The machine failed; customers were turned away. At one point, one of the founders was so angry with the machine, he famously beat it with a hatchet.[28] Sounds cathartic, doesn't it? After this (*ahem*) incident, the founders got to work on making major modifications to the machine, eventually working out its considerable kinks. While many more examples of realizing activities could be provided, the point is that realizing value propositions overlap with but is also distinct from initial exploring activities and that both matter.

Exploring-realizing are a set of entrepreneurial constitutive activities, as indicated by the hyphen. They go together and mutually influence one another directly. Think of it this way: If potential value propositions discovered during exploring activities cannot be realized, then the whole of the constitutive process ends by default. Of course, this book and the SEA model are interested in those value propositions that require the establishment and maintenance of an organization to implement; thus, the exploring-realizing set of entrepreneurial activities is an important starting point for organizational constitution. If potential value propositions cannot be implemented considering social and material realities, no organization is possible, and the constitutive cycle ends before it begins. Another possibility is that no market exists for the good- or service-benefit that was generating during exploring activities. Such a situation will be revealed during realizing activities. In other words, imagine getting a business started and then, *crickets chirping*, no one cares. In which case, attempts at creating a market for the desired benefits might follow. Those exploring-realizing possibilities feedforward and feedback to one another and shape them. Of course, a lack of startup funds or venture capital can be a common reason why exploring is not realized and vice versa.

Given that the communication and entrepreneurship fields have had only modest mutual influence to date, it is important to ask, "Where's communication in exploring-realizing?" Exploring-realizing activities are probably mostly classically associated with widespread mental models of entrepreneurs as an identity. There may be a temptation to conceive of exploring-realizing activities as entirely intellectual, in which a tech genius conceives of a value proposition fully formed without being influenced or needing revision. And, no doubt, intelligence *is* a part of these activities. Exploring activities involve both an understanding of the environment and a spark of creative vision that projects a possible valued benefit. Yet, both will almost always depend on communication. Understanding the environment—available resources, local opportunities, industry changes, and market trends—means communication will be key. Interpersonal conversations with key informants and sensitivity to media reports are just two obvious and common forms of communication that can greatly aid a would-be entrepreneur in the early stages of exploring. Meanwhile, gaining a spark of creative vision that projects a possible valued benefit is often an ongoing process that gets revised and revised again by subsequent realizing activities. Crucially important conversations with friends, family, potential employees and early members, potential landlords, potential vendors, potential customers, potential mortgage lenders, and so forth all feedback into the creative and revisional process that is the articulation of value propositions.

If it is not yet clear, we are explaining that communication—and the learning or failure to learn that it brings—is where the momentum of new organizational constitution occurs. Exploring-realizing activities involve a lot of communication, as both speakers and listeners. Learning about the environment and formulating (and *re*formulating) value propositions needs high-quality communication to succeed. In other words, exploring-realizing can involve any and all of the four constitutive flows described in Chapter 1 (i.e., activity coordination, membership negotiation, institutional positioning, and self-structuring). However, we do not necessarily specify when each is occurring and, instead, focus on the activities of entrepreneurship for organizational constitution while applying CCO theory's assumption that most, if not all, of those activities have a communicative element.

Exploring-realizing is the first pairing of constitutive entrepreneurial activities because they represent a beginning point of new firm creation. They are, perhaps, what we most ordinarily associate with entrepreneurship. On one hand, the quality of being the start of the constitutive process marks it out as distinctive and important. On the other hand, that quality can make individuals tend to overestimate its importance in the constitution of a new firm in the sense that while exploring-realizing are essential and initial, no firm could be established and maintained without the other sets of constitutive activities. Activities that are so diverse and divergent usually demand many individuals to complete them. (See the discussion of distributed constitutive leadership in Chapter 1).

In sum, exploring-realizing involves those entrepreneurial activities that deal with discovering and implementing valued benefits for customers and clients. Exploring-realizing are about those revolutionary second-order organizational changes brought about by entrepreneurial activities that initial new firms. The first set of constitutive activities involves communicating for creatively identifying value propositions and figuring out how those benefits can be brought to market. Exploring-realizing activities generate the first big momentum push for an organization; for something to come from nothing.

Doubting-Updating: Internal Entrepreneurial Activities

The next set of activities becomes relevant after an organization's reason for being has been sufficiently formulated to make it clear that organization is necessary for the realization of a value proposition or propositions. To be clear, there are value propositions that individual entrepreneurs can offer without the need for organization. Consider, for example, the many individual resellers who trade collectibles and other auction items via websites, such as eBay.com. Presumably, an individual could create their own micro-business without the need for hiring members, dividing up labor, and coordinating actions. However, once value propositions are complex enough to require other members, organization is needed. For example, eBay has more than 13,000 members worldwide, generates billions of dollars of revenue every year, and is publicly traded.[29] The establishment and growth of such a large firm needed much more than a single individual offering a single value proposition. In other words, the SEA model deals with those entrepreneurial enterprises that require organization and doubting-updating activities help explain how individuals scale up to organization (and why some fail to do so).

Doubting-updating involves activities that support the rise of the *internal* functioning of an organization. Doubting-updating activities can be numerous: Hiring and firing, developing and modifying procedures, implementing and streamlining technologies and equipment, and divvying up responsibilities appropriately, are just a few. Labeling these activities as, doubting-updating, is intentional in order to imply that establishing a new organization is a messy, chaotic, and often unpredictable undertaking. Many issues must be addressed. Some issues can be anticipated, and some cannot. Some responses will have negative and unintended consequences, and some will not. Doubting-updating activities are all about building momentum and fighting the resistance of static inertia that would deny momentum from taking hold or drag it back to a standstill. Sally Maitlis and Scott Sonenshein's[30] work identified "updating" and "doubting" as key processes that support adaptive learning by teams and organizations during crises. Maitlis and Sonenshein were heavily influenced by social psychologist Karl Weick,[31] who was a profound influence on the modern study of organizational communication. We borrow Maitlis and Sonenshein's work here and extend it into the domain of constituting a new organization.

Admittedly, "doubting" does not sound cheery and optimistic. We understand these internal and organizationally-constitutive activities may be counter-intuitive at first blush. Let us explain: Doubting is about maintaining a mindset of confident uncertainty.[32] To be confident *and* uncertain means to be committed and open to learning and adapting, while at the same time being committed to the notion that learning is indeed needed.

Doubting involves knowing that whatever seems to be working now has at least two very contingent qualities: what (a) *seems* to be working in the early and partial organization[1] could be an illusion and what works (b) *now* in the organization might not continue working into the future. Confidence comes in the form of moving forward and taking opportunities, fixing problems, and anticipating future problems; uncertainty comes in the form of knowing problems and their fixes are bound by perspective and time. A once-for-all fix does not exist. The social psychologist, Ellen Langer, describes this mindset as mindfulness.[32] To notice differences and changes in the organization's internal functioning and the environment goes a long way to being prepared to respond in a healthy, teachable, and let's-try-something-else manner[33,34] by updating.

Consider, for example, the story of the tortilla warmers: A small vendor supply store owner was frustrated to see that a large supply of tortilla warmers was not selling. Tortilla warmers are Styrofoam and oval for packaging tortillas and taking them to-go from a restaurant. The founder lamented his disappointment to the store manager. The warmers sat on the shelves for months. It seemed neither the owner nor the manager could sell them to local restaurants. One day, a customer asked the manager whether the store stocked any worm boxes. Worm boxes are Styrofoam containers that keep fishing bait alive between refrigeration and the hook. Thinking quickly, the manager answered "Yes!" and brought a few examples of the tortilla warmers for the customer's inspection. The customer was pleased with the unique shape and bought the lot.[35] Thinking of the tortilla warmers as tortilla warmers was no longer working. The identification and discussion of the inventory weakness and an openness to new ways of thinking about it,[35,36] that is doubting, prepared the way for a much-needed update.

Updating involves activities that enact changes to ways of doing that make the organization more fit with its environment. They can be big changes or small ones (as with relabeling tortilla warmers). The main point is that updating (up-to-dating) involves the adaptation of the organization to the environment. Updating occurs when we attempt to address weaknesses or invest in current or potential strengths, such that the organization is better able to meet its challenges and fulfill its reason for being. Countless problems and potential problems belong to the constitutive activities of doubting-updating. However, getting coworkers to work together productively and efficiently (i.e., activity coordination), hiring and firing (i.e., membership negotiation), and dividing labor and responsibilities (i.e., self-structuring) will be especially potent in terms of their implications for constituting a new organization (see Chapter 1 description of the four flows model).

To be clear, change itself is *not* the activity of updating. Constantly attempting to implement the most recent management fad can make the organization *less* able to meet its challenges,[37] in part, because management fads often do not update any specific weakness or invest in strengths present in the organization. Change for its own sake is not enough to be considered a constitutive updating activity.

Doubting-updating is a set of constitutive entrepreneurial activities because, as with exploring-realizing, they influence one another. The previous description of doubting and updating may have implied that this process is easy. It is not. Need to create a new organization?: Just learn! Or, more colloquially, "Just fake it 'till you make it!'" We do not intend for that kind of a reading. Doubting-updating are an incredibly difficult set of constitutive activities because of our tremendous limitations as communicators and thinkers. Scholars call our limited capacity to think clearly, bounded rationality.[38,39] As finite creatures, we do not have all the information; we cannot think through all possibilities; we certainly do not know what the future holds. In a word, we are *limited*—thus the need for doubting-updating.

Our limitations are abundant. As communicators in organizations, we have this problematic tendency to engage in cover-ups, such that we avoid discussion of weaknesses, errors, and mistakes, especially if they may be the source of embarrassment for ourselves or powerholders.[22,23,40] We are socialized throughout our lifespan to protect our own public image as well as the public image of authority figures by avoiding or greatly softening discussions that reveal ourselves or others to be at fault, negligent, weak, or in need of improvement.[41] Whether we are aware of it or not, our modus operandi in communication is to engage in self-censorship such that issues that need to be addressed are rendered undiscussable.[23] Yet, if we cannot talk collectively about needed areas of improvement, we cannot think collectively about them and then act collectively to remedy them.[42] We are bounded communicators, indeed. Doubting-updating constitutive activities will have to battle this befuddling tendency toward cover-up communication, which, if left unchecked will render early organizing efforts incapable of being sustained long enough or well enough to become an organization (noun). Once an organization is constituted, doubting-updating activities will remain a key determining factor in whether an organization survives and thrives or whether it declines and dies.

Consider, for example, the following story retold by an anonymous employee about an unlikely and honest conversation that occurred with his bosses—co-owners of a new small business. The employee explained:

> [I] was the manager of a [new] small, local business. The owners—husband and wife—were a bit on the selfish side. I constantly was trying to get them to raise the pay of [the five] employees [who told me they were looking elsewhere for jobs] but [the owners] were standoffish [when I tried to talk to them

about it].... One day in the afternoon... the owner was talking about her kids being in college and how money was tight. She noticed how I made a face when she [made a bad joke] about having to 'Cut back on... buying designer handbags.' I think she realized how ridiculous she sounded to me. It led to a more honest conversation.... It was very earnest... She actually listened.... there were [small-to-moderate] raises.... Over the next couple of months, things got better [and employees stopped looking for other jobs].[43]

The story represents the exception that proves the rule: Rarely do people talk honestly and openly about such sensitive and potentially embarrassing topics. Instead, they grumble, gossip, and gripe to coworkers, family, and friends. Members will tend to either self-censor or act defensively, such that the happy but false storyline that "all is well" continues. In the example, the low pay was threatening the internal functioning of the small business in the sense that its few employees were looking for better paying jobs. With five employees, one could easily imagine a scenario in which two or three employees' quitting simultaneously could quickly spiral out of control if those remaining are overburdened and thereby more motivated to leave too. Yet, thankfully, the owners and manager (speaking on behalf of other employees) were able to engage in doubting communication together; the subsequent updating kept the internal organization functioning moving forward. The example also illustrates how doubting-updating activities were related to membership negotiation (i.e., *maintaining* membership) and how potent that was in keeping constitutive momentum going.

Our limitations as communicators are matched by our limitations as thinkers. For the entrepreneur, the inability to predict the future remains a key limitation. The truth is, we do not know what tomorrow will bring.[44] Certainly, we can make educated and wise guesses, but they remain *guesses*. Prior to the global pandemic, who would have predicted the meteoric rise of teleconferencing technologies (e.g., Zoom, Microsoft Teams)? Conversely, who would have predicted the meteoric fall of massive companies, such as Enron, Nokia, Borders Books, and so many others? Additionally, even when entrepreneurs and their members can envision and implement the delivery of value propositions, the ways they solved logistical and organizational problems will not work forever. The relentless marching on of time means that yesterday's solutions tend to have an expiration date. Doubting-updating activities are necessary because of our limitations as communicators and thinkers. And because the environment in which the organization survives (or fails to do so) is constantly changing and making new demands upon it.

Notice how important feedback is to the doubting-updating process. In the tortilla warmer example and in the difficult conversation about employee wages example above, a signal was noticed: slow-moving inventory or a disproving look from an employee. That signal suggested weakness—weakness which was taken seriously enough to launch a search for a fix. In these examples, weaknesses were identified *retrospectively* via doubting activities. It is important to note that doubting activities can also include identifying potential future weakness *prospectively*.[33,39] What happens to open-heart surgery patients when a hospital loses electrical power to the building? Do patients die? Do the machines keeping patients alive merely stop working? Game over? Nope. Backup generators save the day. Backup generators are the result of prospective feedback in the sense that medical professionals and hospital operations managers asked the question, "What if?" What if the power goes out? The future-oriented and hypothetical feedback along with its answer in terms of a backup plan makes the organization more reliable. In sum, doubting-updating activities do not only pertain to past and current time periods but can also include future and possible periods as well.

Doubting-updating involves those internal organizational activities that deal with identifying internal opportunities or weaknesses that are ongoing or potential with a posture that presupposes the humility to learn. Then, actions are taken to (attempt to) remedy or mitigate those weaknesses to keep the constitutive momentum going. Communicating to detect and correct problems are essential to the early founding of a new organization so that the valued proposition can be delivered. Without these first two sets of activities (exploring-realizing and doubting-updating) no new organization is possible. Despite their critical role, exploring-realizing and doubting-updating are still not sufficient to constitute a new organization because external stakeholders must be involved in the constitution of the new organization.

Legitimizing-Multiplying/Sustaining: External Entrepreneurial Activities

Organizations need inputs from their environment to get started and to survive. Just as humans and plants need oxygen, food, and water to survive, organizations need resources flowing into them.[45] Yet, organizations also need from their environment more than what humans or plants need: a new organization needs widespread perception from stakeholders that an organization exists and should be treated *as* a bona fide organization.[46,47] Is this just one or two people trying to put on a façade of an organization? Should it be taken seriously as an organization? The two categories of external organizational needs (resources and perceptions) are deeply interrelated. When entrepreneurs get stakeholders to take-for-granted that their organization exists and is a recognized entity, then they are much more likely to obtain needed resources, such as venture capital, vendor contracts, bank loans, new members, and customers.[47] People want to know the new organization's complex value proposition(s) can be reliably and ethically offered. If the perception remains that the new entrepreneurial efforts are junior varsity, kid's stuff, or just too amateur, it will be very difficult to generate a positive flow of needed resources into and out from the new "organization."

Legitimizing activities are all about gaining a taken-for-granted consensus from key stakeholders that an organization exists and should be treated as such. At the founding of a new organization or company, those activities are crucial but also nonobvious. Legitimizing-multiplying/sustaining involves those activities that support the rise of the external image of an organization, or its public face. For now, we mention briefly that legitimizing-multiplying/sustaining can involve a wide range of activities: Networking, marketing, advertising, public relations, publicity, social media communications, as well as branding and logo creation—to name a few (for a richer discussion that involves sustaining, see later in this chapter and Chapter 5, Reflection 12). These activities are often oriented toward solving a crucial conundrum of organizational constitution: That crucial conundrum is a bit like the challenge of getting a good job without having any prior experience. Namely, for all but the wealthiest persons, perceptions of legitimacy are usually necessary to obtain needed resources, such as bank loans, vendor credit, and even employees. Yet, without capital, vendors, and employees, it is difficult to gain widespread perceptions that the organization is a bona fide and legitimate organization.[48]

Consider, for example, how skilled tradespersons often begin their own company: A key question for them becomes, "How do we get vendors to loan us materials until we can get paid?" New construction plumbing, electrical, or heating, ventilation, and air conditioning (HVAC) often requires expensive upfront material costs or expensive lease equipment. To be able to establish a new company, these tradespersons need the pipe, fixtures, appliances, wire, ductwork, and heavy industrial equipment provided by large factories and firms. Of course, these factories and firms will not lend thousands of dollars' worth of materials without down payments, collateral, or substantial credit. For those strapped for cash, getting credit with vendors represents a significant barrier to entrepreneurship. Credit with vendors is all about perceptions of legitimacy. Vendors are willing to float large amounts of materials and equipment to business partners with whom they have long and profitable purchasing histories. One common way that skilled tradespersons solve this puzzle is through strategic partnerships (which involve institutional positioning, membership negotiation, and self-structuring communication, see Chapter 1). We know of one such enterprising electrician who agreed to work for a brother-in-law who was already an electrician. The idea was to exchange a portion of his labor for the ability to be associated with, and be seen by, vendors and clients. After several years, vitally important vendors and clients knew and trusted the young man. He was ready to strike out and begin his own company once this crucial conundrum of legitimizing had been solved (for the time being).

This practice (or something similar) is used by many skilled laborers as a springboard for entrepreneurship. Notice how these practices support the idea that legitimizing activities are deeply constitutive of new organizations. They make the difference as to whether an upstart can get needed resource flowing from the environment reliably or not. Once perceptions of legitimacy begin to take hold with the right stakeholders, those perceptions can be exploited to add new members and customers; in turn, more members and customers reinforce a growing taken-for-grantedness that a new organization exists, and the organization is bigger than merely a single skilled worker pretending to be a company. At this point, entrepreneurs and early members will need to make and display symbols that "materialize" the organization—logo, signage, t-shirts, hats, business cards, truck decals, and so many more. These symbols are the visual representation of the new organization that is emerging as a reality.

Multiplying activities are all about increasing precious momentum and staving off constitutive entropy through *growing growth*. Growing growth involves those activities that prioritize additions, which have the potential to add additions. Did you catch the intentional repetition? For example, an individual entrepreneur may increase sales from one month to the next, but such growth is secondary to adding a new salesperson who can multiply (double) growth along with the perception that an organization—not merely an individual—exists and is to be taken seriously. In this way, multiplying activities are about scaling up to and through organization status. Adding is good, but multiplying is great, when it comes to constitutive momentum. Of course, multiplying activities have the potential for rewards and challenges. However, the point is that new organizational establishment is difficult and tenuous. Multiplying activities are therefore especially useful in overcoming the fuzzy and ambiguous developmental period between organizing (verb) and organization (noun).

Sustaining activities are all about maintaining organizational constitution once the organization is taken-for-granted among key stakeholders and in relationship to material resources available. Moving between either legitimizing-multiplying or legitimizing-sustaining (as indicated by the slash) activities is determined by orientation in the organization's constitutive lifecycle. The earlier the entrepreneurial efforts at constituting a new organization, the more multiplying activities are needed. However, multiplying activities can become excessive and outpace exploring-realizing and doubting-updating activities and thereby threaten the existence of a new firm.

Legitimizing-multiplying/sustaining are the only combined set of external constitutive communication because they represent a key feedback loop, which is sensitive to time, material, and lifecycle. As the new organization gains perceptions of legitimacy, obtaining needed resources from the environment will become easier. As resources and perceptions are acquired, gaining more and stronger perceptions of legitimacy will be easier. In other words, institutional positioning will be easier. So too will recruiting and hiring new members (i.e., membership negotiation, see Chapter 1). However, once organization achieves taken-for-granted status and moves from fuzzy, partial organization[18] into a widely-recognized social reality, overdoing multiplying activities can itself become a threat to organizational survival. At that point, legitimizing-sustaining should take over as the primary pair of external constitutive communication. Throughout the lifecycle of an organization, multiplying activities may, indeed, be called for again, after which sustaining activities are needed and so forth.

One way to illustrate the legitimizing-multiplying pairing is to consider the exception that proves the rule: Ever noticed how often celebrity athletes and musicians become entrepreneurs after they achieve fame and financial independence? For example, the professional American tennis phenom, Serena Williams, founded a clothing company, S by Serena,[49] in 2017 after winning more than 20 Grand Slam singles tournaments (among many other professional accomplishments). Her household name status and sizable bank account are tremendously helpful to solving the legitimizing-multiplying puzzle of new organizational constitution. Her name and image are already widely associated with success meaning that obtaining investors, vendors, and customers will be much easier than those who are attempting to start a clothing company without her considerable (and deserved!) acclaim and money (see Chapter 1, description of material resources in organizational constitution). To be clear, the S by Serena company (like all celebrity companies) still had to engage in legitimizing-multiplying entrepreneurial activities to establish their new firm. These celebrity-entrepreneurs just have an advantage in performing these important constitutive activities.

Most of us are not celebrities. Legitimizing-multiplying activities remain difficult without fame and financial backing. Yet, legitimizing-multiplying are no less important in establishing a new company. Consider, for example, the legitimizing-multiplying activities of one of America's earliest and most successful African American female entrepreneurs, Madame C. J. Walker.[50] Born Sarah Breedlove during the post-civil war period, the entrepreneur was orphaned at a young age. By age 22, Breedlove was widowed and needed to care for her daughter. After years of manual labor and poor working conditions, Breedlove began to lose her hair. At the 1905 World's Fair, Breedlove met a businesswoman, Annie Turnbo, who sold cosmetic and hair care products to African American women. Breedlove joined Turnbo and began selling products herself door-to-door enthusiastically. While she learned about the business from Turnbo, Breedlove began experimenting with her own cleansers and perfumes. Eventually, Breedlove got family members to hand-produce her line of cosmetic products, out of her own home.

But Breedlove's dream was much bigger.[50] She wanted her own company, and she envisioned a cosmetic company that would rival any manufacturing company of the time. Yet, getting investors was a substantial barrier for Breedlove's entrepreneurial vision. She wanted a factory and a workforce, which meant she needed significant financial backing. Breedlove did not have enough money to scale-up her operation and business organization. At the turn of the last century, U.S. bankers were reluctant to loan money to women, especially African American women. Breedloves' legitimizing-multiplying activities made the difference. Eventually, she funded a factory *herself.* But not without years of legitimizing activities that slowly grew her personal fortune.

Early in those efforts, Breedlove adopted the moniker, "Madam C. J. Walker." She thought it lent her status—a savvy strategy that functioned to gain perceptions of legitimacy. Madam Walker was a tireless salesperson for her products.[50] She would sell door-to-door personally and traveled away from home weeks. Madam Walker traveled to distant towns to continue individual door-to-door sales because of a need for a larger customer base and associated profit potential. At times, Walker would find temporary work as a cook or maid if she was stranded in a strange town and ran out of funds. Any extra profits were saved and reinvested. For example, Walker was a pioneer in her advertising methods, using Black-owned news-papers to advertise her cosmetic products and using herself as the face of her products. She networked strategically with wealthy Black businessmen and politicians, hosting them for dinners to gain their influence and the legitimacy that came along with having powerful friends. Madam Walker sought out a tutor to improve her communication skills, which would allow her to project an image of education and refinement. Walker lacked formal education but she sought the advice of a trusted tutor on matters of social etiquette, writing, and public speaking.[51]

At the same time as these legitimizing activities, Madam Walker and her family engaged in multiplying activities. Walker hired and trained saleswomen to continue door-to-door sales in several U.S. cities. To facilitate this growth, she created a college to train hair culturists, who would graduate to open new salons and sell Madam Walker products. Additionally, Walker established mail-order op-erations to ensure that new customers, obtained via door-to-door sales, could continue to order her products no matter where they lived. Eventually, Walker saved enough to buy a factory and work-force, a move that solidified her firm. Looking backward, we can see how Breedlove's legitimizing-multiplying activities were admirable and especially pronounced, given the gendered and racial disad-vantages she had to overcome. Later in her career, Walker became a generous philanthropist, humanitarian, and civil rights activist,[50] suggesting her example represents positive deviance worthy of our imitation.

In sum, legitimizing-multiplying involves gaining and sustaining stakeholders' perception that an organization exists and can be trusted. These external activities are similar to and inspired by the four flows model's contention that institutional positioning is essential to organizational constitution (see Chapter 1). Organizational image gets communicated and established in many ways in the minds of stakeholders. A reinforcing cycle is needed such that perceptions and resources build past the critical point of organization (noun) establishment.

Thus far, we portrayed the constitutive activities of the SEA model as being difficult. Indeed, as a rule, they are. Founding a new organization or company is not easy. That challenge means many activities are needed and must be enacted with gusto. Additionally, it will usually mean that more than one person must engage in these activities as they will tend to be too difficult and divergent for one person alone (see Chapter 1), suggesting that constitutive leadership will be distributed among more than one person. Even Madam Walker enlisted the help of her family.

For us, the metaphor of pushing a heavy wheel is apt in that it gives a sense of visceral resistance and movement. To get that wheel moving forward requires a significant and coordinated effort. But the question may be asked: "Is it possible to overdo legitimizing-multiplying constitutive activities? Can constitutive activities be enacted too quickly, too successfully, such that growth is unsustainable and organizational existence is threatened?" The obvious answer is yes. More specifically, unsustainable growth occurs when one or more of the three interrelated pairs of constitutive activities completely outpaces the others. In that sense, the constitutive activities are reciprocal and mutually influencing.

Imagine a scenario in which an authentic Indian cuisine restaurant owner works tirelessly to establish the first location in a small town. The restaurant is slowly gaining in trained staff, customers, positive reviews, and revenues. After two years, the restaurant regularly meets its expenses. Some months turn a profit. A local commercial real estate agent encourages the owner to purchase another location in a nearby town and uses the line, "If you're not growing, you're dying!" On one hand, the additional location could mean a larger loan debt, more travel time between locations, and diverted attention and constitutive activities away from the new organization. Financial strain or a lack of oversight of chef and wait staff could slow down doubting-updating activities, such that customer wait times and food quality decline. Negative word-of-mouth in small towns travels quickly. In that sense, a poorly-timed multiplying activity of opening a second location could undermine legitimizing activities. The decision to expand could represent a threat to the constitution of the first restaurant. On the other hand, depending on material resources and the number of members who can engage in constitutive leadership, the purchase could bolster legitimizing efforts such that a market for the authentic Indian cuisine in the two small towns could mutually reinforce one another and begin to grow both even more. Thus, choosing between legitimizing-multiplying or legitimizing-sustaining constitutive activities are sensitive to organizational lifecycle, available resources, and the degree to which constitutive leadership can be distributed among many members.

Conclusion

In this chapter, we explained the SEA model in greater detail. The emergent property of organization (noun) arises from complex interplays between three sets of activities. The dynamic interplay between these three sets of activities reveals that constituting a new organization is difficult. While substantial money and fame can ease this difficulty, achieving the emergence of a new organization remains challenging. The exploration-realizing of value proposition(s), the doubting-updating of internal functions, and the legitimizing-multiplying/sustaining of the external image require many activities—more than can usually be accomplished by any one single entrepreneur alone.

Notes

1 Bloodletting: Why doctors used to bleed their patients for health. *Medical News Today*. Retrieved from https://www.medicalnewstoday.com/articles/bloodletting-why-doctors-used-to-bleed-their-patients-for-health.
2 Janis, I. L. (1971). Groupthink. *Psychology Today, 5*, 84–90.
3 Hirokawa, R. Y., & Rost, K. M. (1992). Effective group decision making in organizations: A field test of the Vigilant Interaction Theory. *Management Communication Quarterly, 5*, 267–288.
4 Orlitzky, M., & Hirokawa, R. Y. (2001). To err is human: To correct for it divine: A meta-analysis of research testing the functional theory of group decision-making effectiveness. *Small Group Research, 32*, 313–341.

5 Spreitzer, G. M., & Sonenshein, S. (2003). Positive deviance and extraordinary organizing. In K. S. Cameron, J. E. Dutton, & R. E. Quinn (Eds.), *Positive organizational scholarship: Foundations of a new discipline* (pp. 207–224). Oakland, CA: Berrett-Koehler.

6 Spreitzer, G. M., & Sonenshein, S. (2004). Toward the construct definition of positive deviance. *American Behavioral Scientist, 47*, 828–847. doi:10.1177/0002764203260212.

7 See page 281 in Bisel, R. S., Kavya, P., & Tracy, S. J. (2020). Positive deviance case selection as a method for organizational communication: A rationale, how-to, and illustration. *Management Communication Quarterly, 34*(2), 279–296. doi:10.1177/0893318919897060.

8 https://www.usablestats.com/lessons/normal.

9 Bisel, R. S., Kramer, M. W., & Banas, J. A. (2017). Scaling up to institutional entrepreneurship: A life history of an elite training gymnastics organization. *Human Relations, 70*(4), 410–435. doi:10.1177/0018726716658964.

10 Banas, J. A., Bisel, R. S., Kramer, M. W., & Massey, Z. (2019). The serious business of instructional humor outside the classroom: A study of elite gymnastic coaches' uses of humor during training. *Journal of Applied Communication Research, 47*(6), 628–647. doi:10.108 0/00909882.2019.1693052.

11 Sims, R. R., & Brinkmann, J. (2003). Enron ethics (or: culture matters more than codes). *Journal of Business Ethics, 45*(3), 243–256.

12 See page 283 in Bisel, R. S., Kavya, P., & Tracy, S. J. (2020). Positive deviance case selection as a method for organizational communication: A rationale, how-to, and illustration. *Management Communication Quarterly, 34*(2), 279–296. doi:10.1177/0893318919897060.

13 U.S. Bureau of Labor Statistics (2020). *Survival of private sector establishments by opening year.* Retrieved from https://www.bls.gov/bdm/us_age_naics_00_table7.txt.

14 Hait, A. W. (2021, March 29). Women business ownership in America on the rise: Number of women-owned employer firms increased 0.6% from 2017 to 2018. *United States Census Bureau.* Retrieved from https://www.census.gov/library/stories/2021/03/women-business-ownership-in-america-on-rise.html.

15 Women business owner statistics. (2021). *National Association of Women Business Owners.* Retrieved from nawbo.org/resources/women-business-owner-statistics.

16 Preston, C. (2008, November 20). Most small companies make charitable donations. *The Chronicle of Philanthropy.* Retrieved from https://www.philanthropy.com/article/most-small-companies-make-charitable-donations-survey-finds/.

17 Paynter, B. (2018, September 13). Big companies donate a smaller percentage of their income than regular people. *Fast Company.* Retrieved from https://www.fastcompany.com/90233934/big-companies-donate-a-small-percentage-of-their-income-than-regular-people.

18 Ahrne, G., & Brunsson, N. (2011). Organization outside organizations: The significance of partial organization. *Organization, 18*(1), 83–104. doi:10.1177/1350508410376256.

19 Crossan, M. M., Lane, H. W., & White, R. E. (1999). An organizational learning framework: From intuition to institution. *Academy of Management Review, 24*(3), 522–537.

20 Crossan, M. M., Maurer, C. C., & White, R. E. (2011). Reflections on the 2009 AMR decade award: Do we have a theory of organizational learning? *Academy of Management Review, 36*(3), 446–460.

21 Weick, K. E., & Westley, F. (1996). Organizational learning: Affirming an oxymoron. In S. R. Clegg, C. Hardy, & W. R. Nord (Eds.), *Managing organizations: Current issues* (pp. 440–458). London: Sage.

22 Argyris, C. (1980). Making the undiscussable and its undiscussability discussable. *Public Administration Review, 40*(3), 205–213.

23 Argyris, C. (1976). Single-loop and double-loop models in research on decision making. *Administrative Science Quarterly, 21*, 363–375.

24 See page 373 in Cope, J. (2005). Toward a dynamic learning perspective of entrepreneurship. *Entrepreneurship Theory and Practice, 29*(4), 373–397.

25 Cope, J., & Watts, G. (2000). Learning by doing–An exploration of experience, critical incidents, and reflection in entrepreneurial learning. *International Journal of Entrepreneurial Behavior & Research, 6*, 104–124.

26 See page 28 in Schein, E. H. (1993). On dialogue, culture, and organizational learning. *Organizational Dynamics, 22*(2), 40–52.

27 Bisel, R. S. (2017). *Organizational moral learning: A communication approach.* New York: Routledge.

28 Smith, H. (2018, April 18). David Edgerton, Burger King co-founder who helped make the Whopper, dies at 90. *The Washington Post.* Retrieved from https://www.washingtonpost.com/local/obituaries/david-edgerton-burger-king-co-founder-who-helped-make-the-whopper-dies-at-90/2018/04/18/609b2e18-4313-11e8-bba2-0976a82b05a2_story.html.

29 Rathore, S. (2021, February 19). Fascinating eBay statistics and facts for small business sellers. *Small Business Trends.* Retrieved from https://smallbiztrends.com/2021/02/ebay-statistics.html.

30 Maitlis, S., & Sonenshein, S. (2010). Sensemaking in crisis and change: Inspiration and insights from Weick (1988). *Journal of Management Studies, 47*(3), 551–580.

31 Weick, K. E. (1995). *Sensemaking in organizations* (Vol. 3). Thousand Oaks, CA: Sage.

32 Langer, E. J. (2014). *Mindfulness.* Boston, MA: Da Capo Lifelong Books.

33 Weick, K. E., & Sutcliffe, K. M. (2006). Mindfulness and the quality of organizational attention. *Organization Science, 17*(4), 514–524.

34 Vogus, T. J., Rothman, N. B., Sutcliffe, K. M., & Weick, K. E. (2014). The affective foundations of high-reliability organizing. *Journal of Organizational Behavior, 35*(4), 592–596. doi:10.1002/job.1922.

35 Kramer, M. W., & Bisel, R. S. (2021). *Organizational communication: A lifespan approach* (2nd ed.). New York: Oxford University Press.

36 McCaffrey, T., & Pearson, J. (2015, December). Find innovation where you least expect it: How to overcome 'functional fixedness' and other biases that get in the way of creativity. *Harvard Business Review.* Retrieved from https://hbr.org/2015/12/find-innovation-where-you-least-expect-it.

37 Miller, D., & Harwick, J. (2002, October). Spotting management fads. *Harvard Business Review.* Retrieved from https://hbr.org/2002/10/spotting-management-fads.
38 Simon, H. A. (1972). Theories of bounded rationality. *Decision and Organization, 1*(1), 161–176.
39 Simon, H. A. (1991). Bounded rationality and organizational learning. *Organization Science, 2*(1), 125–134.
40 Wright, G., Van Der Heijden, K., Bradfield, R., Burt, G., & Cairns, G. (2004). The psychology of why organizations can be slow to adapt and change. *Journal of General Management, 29*(4), 21–36.
41 Detert, J. R., & Edmondson, A. C. (2011). Implicit voice theories: Taken-for-granted rules of self-censorship at work. *Academy of Management Journal, 54*, 461–498.
42 Bisel, R. S., Messersmith, A. S., & Kelley, K. M. (2012). Supervisor-subordinate communication: Hierarchical mum effect meets organizational learning. *Journal of Business Communication, 49*, 128–147. doi:10.1177/0021943612436972.
43 See pages 211–212 in Bisel, R. S. (2017). *Organizational moral learning: A communication approach.* New York: Routledge.
44 English Standard Version, James 4:13–15.
45 Daft, R. L., & Weick, K. E. (1984). Toward a model of organizations as interpretation systems. *Academy of Management Review, 9*(2), 284–295.
46 Brummans, B. H. (Ed.) (2017). *The agency of organizing: Perspectives and case studies.* New York: Routledge.
47 Taylor, J. R., & Cooren, F. (1997). What makes communication 'organizational'?: How the many voices of a collectivity become the one voice of an organization. *Journal of Pragmatics, 27*(4), 409–438.
48 McPhee, R. D., & Iverson, J. (2009). Agents of constitution in comunidad. In L. Putnam, & A. Nicotera (Eds.), *Building theories of organization: The constitutive role of communication* (pp. 49–87). New York: Routledge.
49 https://www.serenawilliams.com/pages/about-s-brands.
50 Smith, R. Q. (2007). *Madam C. J. Walker (1867–1919). African American entrepreneur, philanthropist, social change agent, and educator of African American women.* [Unpublished doctoral dissertation]. University of Tennessee, Knoxville.
51 See page 98 in Smith, R. Q. (2007). *Madam C. J. Walker (1867–1919). African American entrepreneur, philanthropist, social change agent, and educator of African American women.* [Unpublished doctoral dissertation]. University of Tennessee, Knoxville.

3 Exploring-Realizing Entrepreneurial Activities of New Organizational Constitution

Abstract

New firm creation involves vision and a lot of communication. This chapter provides a closer look at the first set of entrepreneurial activities in the seven entrepreneurial activities (SEA) model, specifically, the interrelated activities of exploring and realizing. On the one hand, these activities are perhaps most associated with the identity of the entrepreneur; yet, descriptions of entrepreneurship can often neglect discussions of organizational constitution. On the other hand, to date, descriptions of organizational constitution often neglect the role played by entrepreneurial visioning and the communication needed to work out value propositions that drive the initial and ongoing impetus for organization. The chapter begins with a brief review of the history of the printing press, which serves as an illustration of the power of entrepreneurial vision in a world of constant change and introduces Dee's experiences in owning a printing company. Then, the chapter presents four autobiographical reflections from Dee's experience as an entrepreneur, which are followed by commentaries that explain where exploring-realizing activities are observable in those stories.

The Printing Press and the Permanence of Change in Business

Historians agree that printing originates in China and Japan hundreds of years before its arrival in Europe.[1,2] The invention of print typographic technology would trigger massive societal changes. Johannes Gutenberg is credited with introducing modern printing and typography to Europe with the mechanical press around 1439. The printing press was both old and new. Modern printing borrowed ancient practices, including Egyptian seal-engraving, Babylonian brick-carving with written language, and Roman ink-printing on

DOI: 10.4324/9781003291312-3

hand stamps.[3] Gutenberg combined these old ideas with a new one: A simple apparatus for making movable type quickly and cheaply.[4] The apparatus is a simple and clever tool, akin to the innovativeness of the pin or needle.[4] The apparatus made movable type, which are small metal pieces with raised backward letters. The movable types get arranged in a frame to spell messages; once arranged, they are coated with ink and pressed firmly to paper. Page after page can be quickly pressed making wider distribution possible. A communication revolution was born. Historians observe that the mass production of publications by the printing press heralded huge societal changes as well as advances in education, religion, literature, philosophy, and politics. "Indeed, it is difficult to overstate the significance of printing as an instrument of change."[5]

The influence of the printing press on world events is matched by few inventions in history, comparable to the global influence of gunpowder and the compass.[6] The communication technology was the result of an entrepreneurial new firm creation: A banker, Johann Fust, invested in Gutenberg's idea, who in turn, hired employees to apply the new technique and technology to copy the Bible.[3] A single operator could not accomplish the massive new feat. Gutenberg opened a shop and assembled employees to work; the organization likely took nearly six years to generate the first copies. Fust's entrepreneurial investment and Gutenberg's organizational constitution efforts were, no doubt, historically significant. Furthermore, the Bible came to be the most reproduced and highest selling book in history[7]—demonstrating that Fust's business hunch was correct. The history of the print business is one marked by the permanence of change—a quality that continues to be reflective of organizations all the more. At the outset of the printing industry, Gutenberg and Fust were engaged in exploring and realizing value propositions (i.e., making and selling copies of the Bible) that required the need for organization.

A major shift in printing technology arrived 500 years later. Movable type gave way to offset printing, which became mainstream globally by the 1960s. Offset printing is a technique in which inked images are transferred from a plate to a rubber blanket and then to paper. Press operators could transfer images to a plate-and-rubber blanket combination using technology like developing photographs. Once an offset press is configured, it can make hundreds or thousands of transfers an hour. The technology increased speed and color options dramatically during the end of the 20th century.

Another massive change arrived with the digital revolution, only a couple of decades later. Digital printing was widely used by the 2010s and made mass-produced publication more possible and personalized. Shorter runs and more colors were more accessible to the average print-buyer. Digital printing uses an imaging process (technically, Raster Image Process) that allows artwork to be transferred directly from digital file to a digital printer. The change means a once industrial undertaking can be accomplished in office settings with quicker turnarounds, brighter and more colors, and without reliance on skilled craftspeople.

Exploring-Realizing

Recall from Chapter 2 that exploring-realizing activities are all about creatively conjecturing value propositions (exploring) and bringing them to fruition despite—or because of—the constraints of reality (realizing). Exploring involves communication with many relevant others about the environment of opportunities, available resources, and future possibilities. Realizing involves communication too, in the sense that value propositions must be implemented in light of real or imagined realities, such as those involving market demands, equipment needs, monetary constraints, among many others. The relationship between the set of entrepreneurial activities is reciprocal. Value propositions are desired benefits that did not exist previously. Yet just because a value proposition can be imagined, does not mean it can be implemented. Thus, this set of entrepreneurial activities is in dynamic tension and interplay. To be clear, the set of entrepreneurial activities can be present at the outset of business ventures where no firm or organization is needed. However, the need for new firm-creation is set in the context of these communicative and decisional activities. Once value propositions become sufficiently complex to deliver, the need for organization arises. Once the need for organization arises, the remaining activities of the seven entrepreneurial activities (SEA) model will also be necessary (see Chapters 4 and 5). In the following paragraphs, Dee provides several autobiographical accounts from her experiences in starting a new company, followed by commentaries that describe where those accounts illustrate exploring-realizing activities.

Foreword to Autobiographical Reflections

A key to starting a company or organization is to surround yourself with people who look for entrepreneurial inspiration. Can you join a group of aspiring entrepreneurs? Can you talk about ideas with others who are on the same kind of hunt? I was blessed to be raised in one such family—a fact that I took for granted for many years. My circles of entrepreneurs were my parents, grandparents, aunts, and uncles. We were a family of what I like to call, "Main Street business owners." The small local shops that form the character of any town.

My grandparents on my mom's side were both business owners. They owned the only diner and bar in their small town in western Kansas. Grandma ran the diner and Grandpa ran an adjacent "beer joint" (as they were called in the 1950s). Their target customers were farmers, ranchers, and farmhands. My grandmother was a great cook and put the "comfort" in comfort food! Grandpa listened to his clientele, as they drank beer, and discussed financial woes. Many were having a hard time making ends meet until Friday's payday. So, grandpa started his own payday loan business out of the bar. My grandparents saw a need for food, beer, and payday loans and filled that need.

My mother was a business owner too. She was a remarkable seamstress, and our family had a need. We needed more money, which is a popular reason to start a small service business. Mom took her talents and figured out a way to make money for our family. My dad built a sewing workshop in our basement. She specialized in upholstery, slipcovers, and draperies. She got so popular that a large department store eventually hired her to do all their work.

My grandfather on my dad's side was a firefighter, so was my dad. My grandpa became alarmed at the number of fires that could have been prevented if more companies and individuals had fire extinguishers. He decided to open a fire extinguisher sales and service company, part time, out of his garage. When they were not working a shift as firefighters, my grandpa and dad ran the extinguisher business. Eventually, Dad bought the business when my grandfather retired. Grandfather saw a need and he filled it. The result was saved lives and property. My dad sold the business to another company, which is now the largest fire equipment company in our state.

As I reflected on the question, "How did you choose to become an entrepreneur and start a printing company?," I realize that my choice of starting a printing company was organic. I trace that back to my family who were a group of people who treated business ownership as a very real option. They found their inspiration from unique skills, part-time jobs, and passions. I just did the same.

Commentary on the Foreword

In the Foreword, Dee reflects on how she came to be an entrepreneur. She points to family influences and experience as major determinants. We may be surprised to find that the starting-point reflection suggests entrepreneurship was an easy and unproblematic option for her; yet her explanation is reasonable. Business ownership (and entrepreneurship) were role-modeled for her by her family for two generations. Scholarship documented many ways family socialization across the lifespan influences career and job pursuits. Family socialization messages even influence what kinds of career and job opportunities individuals can think of as a real possibility for themselves.[8–10] Here, Dee characterizes entrepreneurial exploring-realizing activities as somewhat mundane habits of mind and as emerging from culturally embedded practices within families or groups. Dee's reflection contrasts with the myth of entrepreneurs as genius loners who develop their innovative value propositions from a blank slate.[11] Indeed, such "great man" or heroic theories of leadership and entrepreneurship tend to say much more about the storyteller than the facts of actual history.[12–14]

Dee remarks that her family members were "business owners." Recall from Chapter 2 that she was somewhat hesitant to label herself an entrepreneur and preferred the label of business owner. She reasoned that labeling herself an entrepreneur would be inappropriate because of its associations with the mental model of a tech-savvy, whiz-kid genius—associations with which she did not identify. Similarly, her family opted for the label business owner, even though they are entrepreneurs by definition (see Chapter 1). One possible explanation for this tension over labels involves the recognition that in everyday talk in the United States, working classes are often denied the right to claim entrepreneurial legitimacy.[15] Dee's family members were working class and she likely adopted the vocabulary preference effortlessly.

Dee's communication network served as a backdrop and resource for her formulation of entrepreneurial investigations, curiosity, and sense of possibility. Exploring activities were normalized in her family. Dee's family role-modeled a habit of searching for opportunities and value propositions that could generate profit, making the practice of exploring activities seem commonplace. In the business ventures undertaken by her family, we see that some of Dee's family's businesses required organization (as with the fire extinguisher company), but others did not (as with being an alteration and sewist vendor). Exploring-realizing activities are necessary for either form of entrepreneurial endeavor; once value propositions are sufficiently complex to require organization, then doubting-updating (see Chapter 4) and legitimizing-multiplying/sustaining activities (see Chapter 5) will also be needed.

Autobiographical Reflections of Exploring-Realizing

Reflection 1: *Starting a new business: From nothing to something*
"Wow! It looks great, Dee!"

As corny as it may sound, that comment was something like the moment I decided that printing was my passion. I found a certain joy in helping customers solve problems and printing was my way of doing it.

My first job after college was in a large printing company. After a couple of months of interning, I got hired and promoted to customer service. I enjoyed the process of figuring out how to meet customers' needs. Customer conversations are about getting their vague (and sometimes impossible) printing ideas into a workable solution. Customers are grateful when you can lead them through it.

"Okay, let me ask you some more questions about this project. My job is to get this idea from your head and into your hands," I'd say.

Sure enough, days later, they'd have it in their hands.

"Thank you! Looks great!" Customers are appreciative, sometimes even a little in awe, of the process. I liked that. I worked for that large printing company for seven years doing estimating, purchasing, and sales. At age 30, I was recruited by a large greeting card company to work in management in one of their big production facilities. Over the following 15 years, I worked my way from supervisor to production manager. At one point, I had over 800 production employees, 70 supervisors, and seven department managers reporting to me. The job required skills in leadership, manufacturing techniques, and personnel issues.

So, when the time came for me to explore business ownership. I knew it had to be printing; that was my passion and expertise. But purchasing a printing company required money—a lot of it. That was the first puzzle to solve.

* * *

I knew I needed a business plan to convince a bank to loan me $50,000. So, I worked on writing one up.

If you can believe it, one of my first tasks was getting my husband's agreement to co-sign with me on the business loan. I was shocked to realize that my signature wasn't enough. Bankers required his signature, even on the smallest loans, for the next 20 years, until his death. Fortunately for me, he was committed to supporting me.

A second task was figuring out collateral. When it comes to getting a major business loan, you can only borrow as much as you already have.

While my husband was very supportive of my entrepreneurial dream, his only request was that I never use our home as collateral to obtain a loan. That was tough. So, instead, I used my retirement account. My retirement was 15 years of accumulated profit sharing, which I earned from my work with the greeting card company. With my retirement gambled, there were no safety nets under this high wire act.

A third task was maximizing the benefits I was getting out of my retirement gamble. A problem with using my retirement was that I needed to show the bank that my profit-sharing money could keep my business afloat until it turned a profit. I estimated that I needed two years of cash. Small business survival is unlikely without a lot of upfront cash. I knew it and they knew it. In other words, I needed the retirement money for both loan collateral and business cash. The solution was to withdraw small amounts of the retirement money monthly instead of all at once, that way the balance would remain high enough to secure the loan. Would the workaround work? Time would tell.

A fourth task was to determine which bank to approach for the loan. I wanted a banker who was close and in town. I figured it made sense to use the loan as an opportunity to build a business relationship nearby.

But, that raised the question, "Where should I locate my company?" To answer that question, I hired two consultants to do market research for me. Neither of the consultants knew one another or that I hired two. I gave them the task of identifying what city, within a 60-mile radius, could support a printing company.

"Lawrence, Kansas," was the answer they both gave me. So, I found a banker there.

With these tasks figured out, I hired a certified public accountant to help me compose the business and family plans. The accountant was a task master! She helped ensure that I was answering all the most important questions about finances as accurately as possible.

At that point, I arranged a meeting with a banker. I delivered the business plan days ahead of our meeting so he could read it. When I dropped off the business plan, I decided to include another plan, my family plan.

"I've never seen a family plan before," my banker said at our meeting. "I hope you don't mind, I shared it with a few others. We like it. Great idea, Dee."

The bank agreed to the loan. We would go on to have a wonderful working relationship for many years.

Writing a business plan and getting a bank loan were difficult, but it was the family plan that really spoke to my biggest fear. So, my fifth and the most pressing task was to figure out how my family could survive the loss of my income. You see, at that time, my salary was twice that of my husband's salary. The business plan called for me to avoid taking a paycheck for the first two years; then, I would take only a small salary in the third and fourth years. Yikes! What would it do to my family? Was I nuts!?

So, I decided to do a family plan. I used the same format as my business plan but substituted my family for the business. Here was our situation: Our family income was going to be cut by two-thirds, 66% decrease. To add to the household complication, my husband worked out of town five days a week, our daughter was 16 and our son was 12, we lived in our dream home, and I loved driving a new luxury car. Something's gotta give. The math doesn't add up. Stomach flip.

"Momma is not happy with her job and wants to quit. She plans to start a new business and we are going to figure out how to make it happen. If Momma ain't happy, nobody around here will be happy," my husband announced to our children after calling a family meeting.

The children agreed but I knew they had no idea what they were about to give up.

I went into creative problem-solving mode. I discovered we could rent our house for more than our mortgage payment. We rented out the dream house; we moved into an 800-square-foot apartment in the same school district. My teenagers shared a bedroom for the first time in their lives. Everyone shared a bathroom. We sold the new luxury sedan and bought a used compact car. It took about nine months to write the business plan and family plan and we began the execution of both simultaneously. We did all this before I gave notice at my high-paying management job, which provided the nice lifestyle and retirement that I intended to gamble to follow my entrepreneurial dream.

* * *

About 15 months after I started the company, the Business School at the local university put out a call to local businesses. The call involved partnering with the local university to give seniors an opportunity to audit a business. Senior business majors would audit your company and then offer recommendations as a part of the capstone of their college degree. I always loved education and our university, so I volunteered us.

"Our research team has concluded that your company will close in the next six months," a young man announced to me and my employees as a part of his final project. Gulp.

My employees were completely silent and looked at me with concern. I can only imagine they were updating their resumés in their heads.

"He's wrong, you know," I told them. "His team didn't ask me important questions." I counted on my fingers, "First, they should have asked to review my business plan. They would have seen that the financial reports were exactly as I planned. Losing money in the first two years was planned and the sales targets are right on track. Second, they did not ask if I had any personal capital, in addition to the bank loan, to handle the months of losses. I have retirement money that I planned to use for the first two years, and it's working out as I planned." I gave them a big smile and a wink. They seemed to breathe a sigh of relief.

Going from an idea to an organization—from nothing to something—means finding your team and doing your homework thoroughly.

Commentary on Reflection 1

"Starting a new business: From nothing to something" is an origin story, told from the perspective of an entrepreneur who risks a corporate career, a retirement account, and a comfortable life to begin a new business. (More information on why Dee left her corporate career can be found here[16]). The reflection offers a narrative illustration of the exploring-realizing entrepreneurial activities that precede and initiate an organization. Recall that exploring activities involve conjecturing value propositions—desired goods or services—which can be brought to fruition. Of course, in the case of business organizations value propositions are intended to entice the exchange of money. In the present reflection, Dee spends little time identifying printing as the key value proposition for her entrepreneurial endeavor. She writes with fondness about interacting with printing customers early in her career. Having gained expertise in the practical parameters of printing, she uses her interpersonal skills to guide potential customers through the process of implementing ideas into finished printed materials. Repeated experiences with customers' gratitude indicated to her that customer service and printing are, together, value propositions, which customers want and will pay for. The lion's share of the origin story is less about conjecturing value propositions and more about whether a value proposition (printing) can be brought to fruition through the establishment of an organization, which required a lot of communication and problem-solving about financial challenges and potential family constraints (i.e., realizing). Additionally, Dee's need for an organization to deliver the value proposition of printing is an assumption of her story.

The ease with which Dee identifies printing as a value proposition suggests that exploring activities can be motivated and inspired by past experiences almost effortlessly—a point that is not surprising given the role played by experience and expertise in building intuitive decision-making.[17] Exploring activities are strongly associated with the identity of entrepreneur in the popular imagination: Entrepreneurs tend to be associated with "Eureka!" moments in which an innovation (usually, a technological one[18]) is created from nothing—a process that apparently does occur but is not the only or most common exploring activity.[18,19] Even when eureka moments are a key triggering constitutive entrepreneurial activity, entrepreneurs report that they are only one among many other activities, all or nearly all of which involve communication; they often report that eureka moments emerge after important conversations with others, such as other businesspeople, industry-insiders, and even children.[20]

Dee's company's origin story includes an unexpected innovation that demonstrates a tight association of exploring-realizing activities. The reflection involves the interplay between exploring-realizing activities in the sense that obtaining sufficient loans and financial backing were key reality checks (realizing) that stood in the way of bringing a printing-oriented value proposition to customers (exploring). Notice that money—a material reality[21]—is the key barrier to the realization of her entrepreneurial dream of business ownership—a barrier that represents a "puzzle" (according to her) to be solved. That puzzle is solved through many realizing activities that involve communication, collaboration, and decision-making. One solution involved an innovative strategy of using her retirement account as both collateral for a loan and a source of startup funding. That financial innovation was relatively small and is combined with others, such as hiring important advice-givers (i.e., an accountant and market researchers). Additionally, gaining the consensus of her spouse and children was central to the story. Evidence suggests that women entrepreneurs position the need to balance work and home life to be the most significant constraint they face in business ownership.[21,22] Yet, that constraint is worked through and somewhat resolved as a part of Dee's early exploring-realizing activities. Likewise, scholars noted that successful organizations are usually the net result of many small innovations that get combined in clever ways, and not necessarily the result of a single big idea.[23,24]

The origin story develops around Dee's communication with others in a listwise fashion. Throughout the narrative, we read how she engaged in strategic conversations with her husband and children, two marketing consultants, a certified public accountant, a banker, employees, and even college students. The communicative constitution of her organization is apparent throughout. Other reflections presented hereafter introduce many more key stakeholders and constitutive communication events that were essential in the establishment and maintenance of her new company.

Reflection 2: *Growth opportunity: Acquisition*
*"Hey Dee, calling to see if I can buy you a cup of coffee tomorrow,"
said Jim Nottingham.*

"What a surprise!" I thought. Jim was the owner of Keystone Press, a 35-year-old printing company in my town, that specialized in political printing and bulk mailing. Jim was not the type to attend the Chamber of Commerce or social events, so we had only spoken a few times. I had no idea why he wanted to have coffee, but I was excited to learn why.

The next afternoon we met at a coffee shop and sat outside. After discussing the University's latest basketball win, Jim began, "My right-hand person, Jennifer, announced her retirement and I have been thinking about retiring too." He proceeded, "I thought about all the other printers in town, and I concluded that you would be the perfect match for my employees and customers. Would you consider buying Keystone from me?"

I was flattered and shocked. Gathering my composure, I said, "This is a surprise. I'll give it thoughtful consideration. Of course, I need a lot of information before I make such a big decision."

He agreed and suggested that I visit his shop the following Friday. His employees leave at 3:30 pm. He wanted me to arrive at 4:00 pm.

During the following several weeks we got lawyers, bankers, and finally, our employees involved with the transaction and transition. Jim set the price and his attorney did the contract work.

In retrospect, I made two major mistakes during this process. First, I used my attorney who completed our family trust and not an attorney who specializes in business transfers. Second, I let Jim set the price. I should have hired an independent business appraiser to do a complete analysis of the business and market research on other similar business transactions in the area. Years later, I realized I overpaid when I used a market researcher to set the sales price of my own company. Ouch.

The acquisition represented a 60% increase in our customer list by adding 500+ new customers. It also added a few expensive pieces of equipment and bulk mailing capability. The deal also involved us taking on two new employees. One of those employees was a great addition to our team.

The other employee was Jim's brother, Andy.

"What's that smell?" I asked Andy, finding him outside during a break. I knew it wasn't merely cigarette smoke. No, it was marijuana.

"Uh, just a little weed. It calms me down," he said with a half-smile.

"Well, that might be the case, but it's illegal, it's against company rules, and it makes you a liability around our press machines. It's about safety. Go home and sober up. I'll decide what to do about you tomorrow." He looked stunned, which surprised me because he agreed to a drug test when I hired him.

Andy came to work the next morning. "I don't see what's the big deal," he protested. "I've been smoking weed and running a press for 25 years!"

Apparently, his brother didn't mind it. But I did. Safety is too important. I fired him right then.

A year after the acquisition, I could see the fruits of the deal. The good news was that the acquisition increased our total sales substantially. Exactly what I planned!

The banker set the payments on a sliding scale. Each year the monthly payments would go up 20%. The loan would be paid off in 5 years. Year one was fine and we enjoyed the process of learning how to manage political printing, the challenges of working with politicians, and navigating the post office paperwork. Sales were good. The second year was a bit harder because it was not an election year. Year three was a nightmare! A recession hit and our payments were 40% higher than when we bought Keystone. Sales in all areas took a nosedive. By the time the recession was over, sales dropped back to where they were before we bought Keystone. The payments ballooned and I was providing Jim a monthly salary while I was basically working for free.

When the last payment was made, my staff and I went out into the parking lot and shot off fireworks. My husband had a bottle of champagne waiting for me to celebrate. The Keystone acquisition was a very high-risk decision. My lack of due diligence regarding the price and the contract details were expensive lessons. The risky purchase took several years to pay back. Painful lesson learned.

Commentary on Reflection 2

The reflection, "Growth opportunity: Acquisition," presents difficult lessons learned in exploring-realizing activities. Recall that exploring-realizing activities tend to result in substantial changes and are often the initial impetus for entrepreneurial visions that require organization. Acquisitions usually fit these hallmarks. In the present narrative, an acquisition created substantial changes, which required expanding the organization. With the deal in place, the company greatly expanded its customer list, added new equipment and services (bulk mailing), and resulted in the hiring of two new employees—changes that were certainly not incremental from the perspective of the small business.

Creative conjecturing of a value proposition was assumed and set in advance. It does not take a prominent role in the story; however, it is an important element. The acquired printing company specialized in bulk mailing service, usually connected with political campaigns. Dee takes for granted that there is a market for manufacturing capability, and apparently there was. She knew this from personal and professional experiences interacting with customers and learning about the reputation of her competitors, including Keystone Press. That she could accurately assume these points because of her communication with others in the industry over years. All those conversations were, in retrospect, exploring activities. Here, exploring activities involved both understanding the value proposition presented by the acquisition and having built up the professional reputation and interpersonal relationship with Jim to be offered the deal by him. Thus, Dee's preceding communication with many stakeholders helped her understand the value proposition and receive a growth opportunity where others would not.

These points aside, the main theme of the narrative is somewhat cautionary and offers a reflection on what Dee sees as two critical mistakes (i.e., not obtaining a third-party business valuation and choosing the wrong legal counsel). In the language of the SEA model, these both represent failures of realizing activities. Realizing activities are about the implementation and revision of value propositions. The ideas that form value propositions must be checked, modified, reformulated, or even abandoned considering the constraints of (material) reality. Dee's lament that she allowed Jim to set the price of the acquisition and hired the wrong attorney are retrospective learning moments. These lessons learned are realizing activities that should have reshaped exploring activities. Dee stops short of labeling the entire acquisition as a failure, although her reporting of the consequences of the acquisition is candid (i.e., high payments to Jim with no net increase in company sales). The story of a troubled acquisition is offered in terms of its payoff in lessons. In other words, the difficult-to-quantify return of organizational learning keeps the organization moving forward and reconstituting itself (see Chapter 2).

Reflection 3: *Growth opportunity: Collaboration*

The country was emerging from a recession, and our sales were returning to a profitable level. I had been in a minor car wreck and was having weekly physical therapy. I just finished the weeks' treatments when Michelle, the director of the clinic, stopped me.

"Is your company going to carry the new HIPAA forms?" she asked.

"What are HIPAA forms?" I asked, revealing my ignorance.

Michele explained, "HIPAA is short for Health Insurance Portability Accountability Act. It is a government privacy act that's supposed to protect health information privacy. In theory, it's supposed to make medical information transfers easier and reduce discrimination based on medical information. I'm not sure if it'll actually do those things, but all doctors' offices and hospitals in the country will be required to comply with the new law."

When I got back to work, I began exploring the details of the new act. The color-coded compliant forms were a perfect match for our printing equipment and distribution system. However, we only had about fifty doctors' offices and one hospital as clients.

"Is this worth the investment of time and energy?" I wondered. I needed to put my feelers out, so I called a good friend, Teri, who was the CEO and owner of Medical Systems and Supplies. Her company dealt with medical offices throughout the United States and they had the means to market the forms.

Teri loved the idea of joining forces. If we could get a jump on the competition, we could be a key vendor for doctors and hospitals in the region.

The following week, Teri and I were sitting together at an American Business Women's Association (ABWA) luncheon. Brenda, a local attorney, was the speaker. She was explaining to the crowd of businesswomen that she just returned from a training seminar in California where she got certified as a HIPAA trainer. It felt like the universe was talking to us. We had to get Brenda involved in our new venture.

Teri and I cornered Brenda after lunch and told her what we were doing. Brenda joined our entrepreneurial endeavor and we added HIPAA seminars to our business plan. Admittedly, the plan was a bit unusual. We didn't need a loan or to convince investors. The plan was more of a flow chart that specified how orders, production, seminars, distribution, and payments would move between our respective companies.

The beauty of the entrepreneurial collaboration was that there was very little investment needed. We already had the systems, equipment, and employees in place. We were up and running in three months. Teri's customers were ordering. Brenda was getting us new customers via her seminars. We were easily keeping up with production and distribution. The business plan worked, and new business was coming in for all three of us.

Sales started drying up six months into our new venture. Brenda was canceling seminars for lack of reservations. We met for dinner and drinks to discuss. We decided Teri would call her biggest customers and ask why.

Teri reported back to us later that week. "I'm hearing from my doctors' office clients that they don't think they'll comply with all the 15 different details of the act. They're creating one form—not the 15 forms—and calling it good. They say, 'All these forms are slowing down check-in and besides it's not like there's a HIPAA police.' They are all talking to one another and concluding that they only need one form. Seems that doctors' offices everywhere are doing it this way."

Doctors' offices were using a single form that implied patients had read 15 pages of HIPAA rights and rules. They were also copying that one form on their copiers, with no regard for the copyright. Without visible federal enforcement, the entire act had been reduced to one piece of copied paper.

Ugh. I can't say I blame anyone, but it didn't bode well for our new business.

But that's business.

The HIPAA collaboration was ultimately short-lived and unsuccessful; however, it cost me very little cash, unlike the Keystone acquisition (see Reflection 2). By trying an expansion via a strategic collaboration that used our existing equipment, employees, and distribution system, there was little risk.

Commentary on Reflection 3

Reflection 3, "Growth opportunities: Collaboration," resonates with Reflection 2 in several ways. Both involve key interpersonal relationships that serve as high ground from which to scan the environment for opportunities. In the story, a director knew Dee's professional reputation well enough to approach her as a potential vendor for HIPAA forms. That conversation was only possible because of previous interactions, which established interpersonal connection and their respective personal and professional public images. Dee responds to the inquiry quickly by identifying and communicating with a key member of her professional network (i.e., Teri) whom she believes will be able to provide greater insight into the potential customer request. These conversations are exploring-realizing activities. Dee was noticing cues in her social environment and investigating communicatively and creatively through which a value proposition was able to be articulated. The conversations helped formulate the idea that a collaboration to produce HIPAA forms might be a value proposition for a new market, recently established by federal legislation. Brenda's inclusion in the collaboration is another example of exploring-realizing activities on the part of all three entrepreneurial collaborators.

The trio considered their collaboration to have strong potential in terms of their ability to implement (i.e., realizing) the conjectured value proposition. With little upfront costs, the women saw the HIPAA form business as low risk. Their access to employees and equipment could be relied upon to realize their vision. In other words, in theory, they saw few of the ordinary organizational and material barriers preventing them from establishing a viable business. Yet, institutional forces that they conjectured would give rise to a market for their value proposition, eventually did the opposite, and dissolved the market demand for HIPAA forms. Research in sociology and organizational communication confirm that organizations within an industry (such as the medical field) will tend to behave similarly due to institutional forces.[25–29] One such institutional force involves the influence of governmental regulations on organizations within a country (i.e., coercive isomorphism[24]). Governments can regulate organizations through laws; in turn, those laws can make organizations behave similarly. The collaborators saw the HIPAA laws as likely to produce a market of healthcare organizations attempting to comply with the new law. New customers would be clamoring for their goods, if only they could get a jump on the competition and figure out the logistics.

However, another institutional force can also be in play: The institutional force of mimicry.[25] Organizational decision-makers are motivated to be seen as legitimate by other organizations in their field and key stakeholders[25] (see Chapter 5). That motivation drives them to study and imitate other organizational entities they perceive as legitimate, thus resulting in industries where most organizations look similar.[26,29] In the story, healthcare organizations mimicked one another's utilitarian approach to complying with the federal act and the market for HIPAA forms came to a rapid end. That rapid end meant the entrepreneurs' newly-formed organization was over before it really began. Organizational constitution ended by default. There was no need for internal (i.e., doubting-updating activities, Chapter 4) or external organizing efforts (i.e., legitimizing-multiplying/sustaining activities, Chapter 5) because exploring-realizing activities did not warrant the need for further organization. The lack of market demand meant the value proposition was not valuable after all.

Here again, Reflections 2 and 3 are similar. Both reflections describe entrepreneurial failures. Notice also however that both narratives explain failure in a self-forgetful and self-forgiving way. Within these stories, we can readily identify Dee's humility in that failure is remembered and reported candidly. However, on the other hand, that humility in reporting failures does not result in an unhealthy avoidance of continued exploring-realizing activities; Dee seems to avoid future "analysis paralysis"[30] by ascribing valuable lessons and organizational learning to these efforts, which are hard-to-quantify payoffs that serve as a narrative resolution,[31] even when entrepreneurial success by the standards of long-term survival and profitability are absent. Interestingly, research indicated that little entrepreneurship education is devoted to discussing and learning from failures, despite that entrepreneurship is a complex process necessitating trial-and-error with a high probability of frequent failures.[32,33]

Reflection 4: *The industry leaves "Big Iron"*
"Hello, Mrs. Bisel. This is Sally Jenkins from Globe Press. I work in the Human Resources department. Do you have a minute to talk?" Globe Press was a very large printing company located in a small town about 15 miles away.
"Sure, how may I help you?" I asked.
"Tomorrow, the newspaper will announce that our plant is closing at the end of the month. I was asked to call all the local printing companies and see whether they have any job openings. We hope to help our employees find new employment," she said.
"As a matter of fact, I do have an opening for a press operator, possibly two, if they have a lot of experience and can start immediately," I replied.

Keith and Jeff worked at Globe Press for many years. Ms. Jenkins gave them my contact information. They applied together and were insistent on being interviewed together. That was a first for me. They worked together for over 20 years and were an employer's dream team. I learned from the newspaper article that Globe declared bankruptcy, stating that the market was shifting to newer technologies that could manage shorter runs, quicker lead times, and more color options.

"Globe Press was going the way of the dinosaur," I thought to myself, "I need to make sure that's not going to be us."

Keith and Jeff specialized in an older, traditional form of printing press that we, in the printing business, call "Big Iron." Their press was a city block long and so tall that stairs are needed to get to a platform for hanging printing plates and for inking rollers. Once up on the platform, they would stay for the entire production run. Minimum production runs were 100,000 impressions. A million-impression run was not unusual. Those were the days when customers ordered press runs that would produce enough inventories to last six to 12 months. Keith and Jeff were truly skilled at their craft; unfortunately, no more companies in our region needed those skills.

"Here's the duplicator presses you will be operating," I told them during the interview and tour of the facility. Duplicator presses are the size of a bedroom dresser, at most. They seem almost dainty in comparison to the big iron of their careers.

"That's it?" Keith said with a slight laugh, holding the back of his neck as he shot a sideways look to Jeff. "You sure you need press operators?"

I could read their embarrassment and deep hesitation. Their egos were having a hard time coming to grips with the emasculation of running such small presses. Also, I'm not sure they were immediately happy about the idea of working for a woman. I found myself selling them on the fact that they would have less physical demand on their bodies and much more variety throughout the workday because of short runs and constant color changes. I offered them the same hourly pay as they were getting at Globe Press.

"We'll get back to you," Keith said on their behalf. They shook my hand and forced a smile. I can only imagine they went to the bar to have a drink and talk it over.

Two days later Keith called and accepted the jobs for them both. Keith and Jeff ran the little offset presses for the next 15 years and came to enjoy it—a fact that still makes me laugh a little.

* * *

After a few years of working with small duplicator presses, I made a bold decision to get out of the offset printing business and go to 100% digital printing. Keith and Jeff would have to learn. I was determined we would not go the way of the Globe "Press-asaurus."

After a lot of discussions with employees and a lot of homework, we decided to go all digital and sell the little presses. Going digital was the last step in becoming a completely green printing shop (see Chapter 4, Reflection 8).

I assured Keith and Jeff that they still had jobs with me and that their pay would not change. They were both nervous about being re-trained or being moved to another department.

Digital printing involves computers. They were nervous about their ability to learn the new technology that was replacing their craft. In fact, Keith did not even own a mobile phone.

Our younger graphic designers were very comfortable with the de-cision. We leased a digital press five years before, to start the learn-ing process. They adapted to it easily and it produced beautiful work. Customers loved it. Digital presses meant shorter runs, vivid colors, and quick turnaround—just what the market was demanding.

However, the financial risk was huge. I wanted to retire in less than five years. At that moment, I had no debt, which made retirement feel more possible. In the end, I decided to invest in digital printing any-way. My decision was based on giving customers what they wanted— not what I wanted, which, of course, was to stay debt free. I reasoned that becoming obsolete was worse than taking on debt.

* * *

I smile when I think back about how orders were placed with us when we first opened. People called or walked into the shop. We had to have a full-time person to answer the phone and work the front counter. Our simple management system consisted of a Compaq desktop com-puter and basic software for estimating, job ticketing, and invoicing. A dot matrix printer cackled throughout the day, churning out tickets and invoices for customers.

The current owner, my daughter Kristi, and her staff embraced the latest in technology. When they were shut down for the Covid-19 pan-demic they did not miss a beat. Everyone worked from home and were able to access computer systems. They could communicate with their customers, do estimates, and write orders.

The graphic designers produced copies and got proofs confirmed by customers electronically. When the orders were ready to produce, they would send the graphic design and orders directly to the digital presses—all from their kitchen tables. When they had 3 or 4 jobs completed, they would drive to the shop, finalize the jobs, and deliver them on their way home. Amazing!

Commentary on Reflection 4

Reflection 4, "The industry leaves 'Big Iron,'" illustrates the point that exploring-realizing activities are *ongoing throughout* organizational constitution and are not only the impetus for organizational constitution. The story speaks to the evolving nature of the meaning of value propositions and their implementation across time. Yesterday's value proposition can become worthless in today's world. Popular business press writings often invoke the analogy of buggy whip manufacturers as a business that failed due to obsolescence in the face of technological advancements.[34] While the analogy is somewhat inaccurate and anachronistic,[35] the spirit of the point resonates, which explains its continued usage in corporate settings and business discourse.[36–38] Reflection 4 involves the print industry's version of technological advancement that threatens organizational dissolution. Dee observes a powerful competitor who chose to shut its doors rather than adapt to new market demands for products that no longer required the equipment, termed "big iron." She vows to avoid the mistake and adapt, even at the cost of going further into debt before her planned retirement.

As the nature of value propositions evolve, so too will entrepreneurial activities in order to stave off entropy and keep organizational momentum moving. "Big iron" presses, and the technology they represented, were tremendous innovations in their day. The speed and volume of printing that were made possible by these behemoth machines were highly prized by companies and organizations who saw the printed materials as legitimizing, professional, and cost-effective ways of buying printed goods in bulk. Mass production and distribution of corporate communiques were made possible by them. However, the rapid acceleration of technological advancements seen across the 20th century came to the printing industry, creating a scenario in which Dee's company had to adapt to radical change or risk decline and dissolution. New technologies changed market demands, which inevitably changed the meaning of the printing company's value proposition. To avoid obsolescence, the company undertook a process of evolving its value proposition radically through ongoing exploring-realizing activities. Notice, for example, that Dee purchased a new digital press well before the company changed over the entirety of the company's equipment. Conversations with others in the industry and customers led to a growing suspicion that the digital press technology represented a future reality to which they needed to adapt or die. The early learning paid dividends as employees got comfortable with the equipment.

Less abstractly, the narrative illustrates some of the practical challenges involved with ongoing exploring-realizing activities of organizational constitution. Keith and Jeff's roles in the story represent the cultural and gendered barriers to the easy adoption of new technologies—practical pressures that are often left out of abstract descriptions of technological adaptations in organizational settings and descriptions of the future of work. Keith and Jeff's careers with other printing companies were set within the context of value propositions that were fading into history. Their careers were also set within the context of cultural notions of masculinity that were fading into history. They had to work through the identity-threatening nature of these changes and adapt as employees or risk being (locally) unemployable in their industry. Dee's conversations with the press operators about the technological change were an aspect of the company's ongoing realizing activities. Dee and her employees had to negotiate cultural and gendered barriers for the updating of the company's value proposition (i.e., exploring) to be possible. In doing so, the company ultimately found a reformulation of its value proposition via new technologies, which helped it maintain constitutive momentum to the present day.

Conclusion

This chapter explained and illustrated the first set of entrepreneurial activities of the SEA model—exploring-realizing activities. The SEA model is a prescriptive model of new firm constitution. Exploring-realizing activities are all about articulating and rearticulating value propositions considering material realities and market demands. The chapter began by reviewing the history of the printing industry briefly because the communication-based industry symbolizes the permanence of change in organizations, especially business organizations. Gutenberg and Fust's entrepreneurial collaboration illustrates the point that the impetus for new firms come from those value propositions that require organization to implement them. Yet, the history of the printing industry—with all its technological changes—also suggests that the exploring-realizing activities needed to articulate viable value propositions must be on-going and subject to frequent revision if organizations will survive over the long term. Four autobiographical reflections by an entre-preneur and printing business owner illustrate the big and small ways that communication among diverse and distributed stake-holders is part of the communicative constitution of organizations.

Notes

1 Luckombe, P. (1771/1965). *The history and art of printing*. London: Gregg Press.
2 Palmer, S. (1733/1972). *A history of printing*. New York: Burt Franklin.
3 Winship, B. P. (1968). *Gutenberg to Plantin: An outline of the early history of printing*. New York: Burt Franklin.
4 DeVinne, T. L. (1969). *The invention of printing*. New York: Francis Hart.
5 See page 88 in Taylor, P. M. (2003). *Munitions of the mind: A history of propaganda from the ancient world to the present day* (3rd ed.). Manchester: Manchester University Press.
6 Taylor, P. M. (2003). *Munitions of the mind: A history of propaganda from the ancient world to the present day* (3rd ed.). Manchester: Manchester University Press.
7 Radosh, D. (2006, December 18). The good book business: Why publishers love the Bible. *The New Yorker*. Retrieved from https://www.newyorker.com/magazine/2006/12/18/the-good-book-business.
8 Gibson, M. K., & Papa, M. J. (2000). The mud, the blood, and the beer guys: Organizational osmosis in blue-collar work groups. *Journal of Applied Communication Research, 28*, 68–88. doi:10.1080/00909880009365554.
9 Lucas, K. (2011). The working class promise: A communicative account of mobility-based ambivalences. *Communication Monographs, 78*(3), 347–369. doi:10.1080/03637751.2011.589461.
10 Kramer, M. W. (2010). *Organizational socialization: Joining and leaving organizations*. New York: Polity.
11 Mochari, I. (2014, July 2). The myth of the lone genius entrepreneur. *Inc.com*. Retrieved from https://www.inc.com/ilan-mochari/entrepreneur-lone-genius.html.
12 Fairhurst, G. T. (2007). *Discursive leadership: In conversation with leadership psychology*. Thousand Oaks, CA: Sage.
13 Fairhurst, G. T., Jackson, B., Foldy, E. G., & Ospina, S. M. (2020). Studying collective leadership: The road ahead. *Human Relations, 73*, 598–614. doi:10.1177/0018726719898736.
14 Bisel, R. S., Fairhurst, G. T., & Sheep, M. L. (2022). CCO theory and leadership. In J. Basque, N. Bencherki, & T. Kuhn (Eds.), *Routledge handbook of CCO* (pp. 297–309). New York: Routledge.
15 Gill, R. (2014). 'If you're struggling to survive day-to-day': Class optimism and contradiction in entrepreneurial discourse. *Organization, 21*(1), 50–67. doi:10.1177/1350508412464895.

16 Bisel, D. L., & Bisel, R. S. (2020). Gossip, a leader's cowardice, and a glass ceiling experience. In R. Bisel, & M. Kramer (Eds.), *Cases in organizational communication: A lifespan approach* (pp. 153–157). New York: Oxford Press.

17 Salas, E., Rosen, M. A., & DiazGranados, D. (2010). Expertise-based intuition and decision making in organizations. *Journal of Management, 36*, 941–973. doi:10.1177/0149206309350084.

18 Goodwin, M. (2015, January 9). The myth of the tech whiz who quits college to start a company. *Harvard Business Review.* Retrieved from https://hbr.org/2015/01/the-myth-of-the-tech-whiz-who-quits-college-to-start-a-company.

19 Bolton, B., & Thompson, J. (2004). *Entrepreneurs: Talent, temperament, technique* (2nd ed.). Amsterdam: Elsevier.

20 Expert Panel, Young Entrepreneur Council. (2019, March 20). Eight entrepreneurs share their unique "Eureka!" moments. *Forbes.* Retrieved from https://www.forbes.com/sites/theyec/2019/03/20/eight-entrepreneurs-share-their-unique-sources-for-eureka-moments/?sh=4dc91e111136.

21 Bruscella, J. S., & Bisel, R. S. (2018). Four flows theory and materiality: ISIL's use of material resources in its communicative constitution. *Communication Monographs, 85*(3), 331–356. doi:10.1080/03637751.2017.1420907.

22 Gill, R., & Ganesh, S. (2007). Empowerment, constraint, and the entrepreneurial self: A study of white women entrepreneurs. *Journal of Applied Communication Research, 35*(3), 268–293. doi:10.1080/00909880701434265.

23 Ismail, M. (2005). Creative climate and learning organization factors: Their contribution towards innovation. *Leadership & Organization Development Journal, 26*, 639–654. doi:10.1108/01437730510633719.

24 Burkus, D. (2014). *The myths of creativity: The truth about how innovative companies and people generate great ideas.* San Francisco, CA: Jossey-Bass.

25 Meyer, J. W., & Rowan, B. (1977). Institutionalized organizations: Formal structure as myth and ceremony. *American Journal of Sociology, 83*(2), 340–363.

26 Greenwood, R., & Suddaby, R. (2006). Institutional entrepreneurship in mature fields: The big five accounting firms. *Academy of Management Journal, 49*, 27–48.

27 Lammers, J. C., & Barbour, J. B. (2006). An institutional theory of organizational communication. *Communication Theory, 16*, 356–377. doi:10.1111/j.1468-2885.2006.00274.x.

28 Lammers, J. C. (2011). How institutions communication: Institutional messages, institutional logics, and organizational communication. *Management Communication Quarterly, 25*, 154–182. doi:10.1177/0893318910389280.

29 Bisel, R. S., Kramer, M. W., & Banas, J. A. (2017). Scaling up to institutional entrepreneurship: A life history of an elite training gymnastics organization. *Human Relations, 70*, 410–435. doi:10.1177/0018726716658964.

30 Huberman, E. (2017, May 10). Keep moving or die: 3 tips to prevent analysis paralysis. *Entrepreneur.* Retrieved from https://www.entrepreneur.com/article/293301.

31 Heinze, I. (2013). Entrepreneur sense-making of business failure. *Small Enterprise Research, 20*, 21–39. doi:10.5172/ser.2013.20.1.21.
32 Alvarado Valenzuela, J. F., Wakkee, I., Martens, J., & Grijsbach, P. (2020). Lessons from entrepreneurial failure through vicarious learning. *Journal of Small Business & Entrepreneurship*, 1–25. doi:10.108 0/08276331.2020.1831839.
33 Cope, J. (2011). Entrepreneurial learning from failure: An interpretative phenomenological analysis. *Journal of Business Venturing, 26*, 604–623. doi:10.1016/j.jbusvent.2010.06.002.
34 Levitt, T. (1960/2008). Marketing myopia. *Harvard Business Review* (Classics). Boston, MA: Harvard Business Press.
35 Stross, R. (2010, January 9). Failing like a buggy whip maker?: Better check your simile. *The New York Times*. Retrieved from https://www.nytimes.com/2010/01/10/business/10digi.html.
36 Warner, C. (2013, December 19). The news business and buggy whips. *Forbes*. Retrieved from https://www.forbes.com/sites/charleswarner/2013/12/19/the-news-business-and-buggy-whips/?sh=41b6e1fe664e.
37 Okhuysen, G. A., Lepak, D., Ashcraft, K. L., Labianca, G., Smith, V., & Steensma, H. K. (2013). Theories of work and working today. *Academy of Management Review, 38*, 491–502. doi:10.5465/amr.2013.0169.
38 Cheney, G., Christensen, L. T., Conrad, C., & Lair, D. J. (2004). Corporate rhetoric as organizational discourse. In D. Grant, C. Hardy, C. Oswick, & L. Putnam (Eds.), *The Sage handbook of organizational discourse* (pp. 79–103). Thousand Oaks, CA: Sage.

4 Doubting-Updating Entrepreneurial Activities of New Organizational Constitution

Abstract

New firm creation involves a lot of problem-solving and coordination in communication. This chapter provides a closer look at the second set of entrepreneurial activities in the SEA model, specifically, the interrelated set of activities of doubting and updating. Doubting and updating involve those ongoing efforts to modify and improve internal operations. Recall that exploring-realizing activities set and reset value propositions taking into account material realities and, at times, those value propositions require the founding of a new organization. When and where new organization is needed to implement value propositions, doubting-updating activities will be needed also. Without them, an organization will never exist or will soon cease to exist. Doubting-updating activities can involve a wide range of tasks, from recruiting, hiring, and firing team members, to changing software and standard operating procedures, to shopping for better deals on products and vendors—the aggregation of these incremental activities comes to be the organization's internal operations. When doubting-updating activities are ignored, delayed, or poorly implemented, the organization fades definitionally as it loses fitness with its environment. When doubting-updating entrepreneurial activities are absent or poorly managed, entrepreneurs and early members will have difficulty creating constitutive momentum. The same is true for established organizations that fail in their doubting-updating activities over time.

Recall that doubting-updating activities involve ongoing efforts to notice difference and deviation in the organization's internal functioning and respond with remediation when needed. In other words, we should put a solution in place as we realize we are falling short.

DOI: 10.4324/9781003291312-4

In the organizational realm, those solutions are often routines. Scholars observed that organizations are especially good at establishing routines.[1–4] Routines are standard and repeatable processes that can be applied again and again. They make the world seem much more comprehensible, expected, and predictable.[3,4] Routines are a wonderful way of easing the challenges of the present by applying solutions from the past. However, the advantages of routines also come with substantial disadvantages to organizational constitution. What are those disadvantages? Routines can keep members from recognizing differences that matter, such as change in operations, customers, or the organizational environment. A mindless reliance on past practices, procedures, and policies can create complacency in which we think we have seen and said it all; meanwhile, in reality, small changes in operations, customers, or the environment are making yesterday's routines less and less applicable.[5–7]

To be clear, organizational routines are helpful and virtually impossible to avoid. Thus, the answer is not to avoid routine, but to routinize doubting and updating activities. (We are grateful to Sally Maitlis and Scott Sonenshein for coining these terms[7]). Doubting and updating entrepreneurial activities avoid existential threats posed by complacency. Would-be entrepreneurs, like all humans, tend to fall into complacency and arrogance,[8] often preferring to believe that they have the situation figured out and it will all be okay. That storyline soothes the ego and anxieties, but, over time, it can also make (new) organizations fall into disrepair and further out of step with needed adaptations and improvements.[8–10] Entrepreneurs and organizational members have huge limitations as both thinkers and communicators.[11,12] That quality means doubting and updating activities are needed for new organizations to both present themselves to stakeholders *as an organization* and to avoid fading definitionally and existentially over time. Such observations are important to the communicative constitution of organizations theory (see Chapter 1) because it reiterates that constitutive leadership is likely too complex and multifaceted to be accomplished by a lone individual entrepreneur.[13] In other words, constitutive leadership is distributed across many members and not reducible to the doing or being of a single, lone-creator entrepreneur.[14]

In the following section, Dee provides several autobiographical reflections from her experiences in starting a new company, followed by commentaries that describe where those accounts illustrate doubting-updating activities.

Autobiographical Reflections of Doubting-Updating

Reflection 5: *Hiring (and stealing) rockstar employees*

The old saying, "The customer is always right" is incorrect. Reliable employees are way more valuable and rarer than customers; good leadership will cherish good employees. Over the years, a few customers learned the hard way that treating any of my team with disrespect would result in needing to find a new print vendor. My philosophy was that it is okay to fire customers if they dared to mistreat employees.

Why do I feel so strongly about this topic? Excellent employees are hard to find. It is even harder to find members who strive to grow and adapt along with the business and industry. Putting together a team of outstanding employees is a matter of first importance. Sometimes that requires stealing great employees and sometimes that requires investing in them even when you are short on funds. The point is this: Do what it takes to get and to hold onto rockstar employees.

* * *

"Ernie, I would like to hire you away from Copier City. I don't have a clue how much money you make, but I guarantee I will match it and give you a raise within 90 days. I know you are working at least 60 hours per week. You will work 40 with me for the same salary," I said with a smile. Ernie was an all-around employee rockstar. He was the graphic designer, office manager, and jack-of-all trades for an important vendor. Time and time again, Ernie impressed me. So, I made my move, and made him an offer.

Ernie seemed surprised by my proposal. "Oh! Um, okay. Let me talk to my wife tonight and I'll get back with you," he said.

It was a Friday night and I stopped on my way home to offer him a job right there in the lobby of Copier City. I could see his exhaustion. He worked up to 12 hours per day regularly and was often scheduled for both weekend days.

Ernie was in his mid-twenties, married, and had a young daughter at home. I could not afford a graphic designer on my staff that first year, so we outsourced our graphic design work to Ernie at Copier City. That meant he was already familiar with us and our regular customers. The working relationship meant I had a front-row seat to view his hard work, professionalism, ethics, computer skills, artistic ability, and customer service.

To my delight, I got a phone call that same evening from Ernie. He discussed the job offer with his wife. "Yes, I will take the job. I will need to give two weeks' notice to Copier City on Monday. Is that all right?" he asked.

"Absolutely, I would have it no other way." I replied. His question only confirmed that I was making the right move.

My delight was, in part, fueled by the fact that I experienced so many lousy employees in my many years in corporate management and again in my first year in business.

New businesses often have a specific kind of employee-recruitment challenge: The pool of applicants tends to be individuals that competitors have terminated or laid off for poor productivity, attendance, or work quality (or all three). Therefore, finding good team members and employees is a big challenge that must be solved. The success or failure of the whole business depends on it.

Ernie walked into the shop at 8:30 am Monday morning. "I'm ready to work," he said with an overwhelmed look. "I gave notice at Copier City, and they got pissed. Told me to leave and never come back."

I studied his face for a moment and an idea popped into my head: "Your first assignment is to go home and take a week's worth of paid vacation. Come back next week and we'll get started."

He seemed relieved to get some rest. Soon after Ernie started, I paid for him to stay in Long Island, New York for two weeks of training. He was overjoyed at the chance to travel.

Ernie and I worked together for the next 24 years, until my retirement. He now works with my daughter, Kristi, and is her mentor. He never stopped learning and trying new things. He was the first to study and recommend new production technology and software. He has an uncanny ability to get technicians to teach him how to troubleshoot equipment, so he rarely asks twice for help with the same problem. Customers love him and vendors respect him for his knowledge and expertise.

Success in business is simply not as likely without rockstar employees like Ernie.

* * *

"Dee, this guy, Bill, is the real deal. We're devastated to see him leave. You need to hire him," said Sam, the owner of a printing company in California. Bill worked for him the last ten years and was moving to town so his wife could attend graduate school at the University.

"Ah, I don't have an opening and I can't afford another employee right now," I said.

Sam continued to push, "Look, Dee, you cannot afford to pass on this hire. This is a rare opportunity to get an employee who is completely trained and can do every single job in your shop. Did I tell you he is an award-winning graphic designer, too?"

We were in the middle of a recession and sales were at a three-year low. Hiring him would mean that something would have to give—that something would be my salary. I took a few days to think about it and concluded that, despite the financial pain, it was a good investment. I offered Bill a job. I hired another rockstar.

Like Ernie, Bill is an avid student, an amazing graphic designer, and capable of operating all our equipment. However, Bill's super-power is his ability to see problems before they happen; he figures out how to prevent problems before they happen.

* * *

"You may have noticed I've been out of the workforce for 10 years. I've been a stay-at-home mom and sports cheerleader. You see, I have three very athletic kids and my husband is the head basketball coach at the high school," Katie said with confidence and a smile as I re-viewed her resume. I noticed the gap in employment but was glad to have her explanation.

We needed a part-time graphic designer and equipment operator. So, I ran an advertisement in the local newspaper. I received 110 appli-cations. Katie was the only one who showed up personally and asked for an appointment with me. I liked her personable style, so I hired her.

Katie is, indeed, a skilled graphic designer and equipment operator but her superpower is initiative.

Over the months and years, she made large format printing of her domain. Large formatting printing is great for yard signs and busi-ness banners. She learned the press inside and out.

Perhaps even more impressive, she used her large network of sports contacts to tell people about the press and what it could do. Orders poured in.

During the early months of the pandemic, Katie's initiative was on full display. She hatched a plan to offer "Congratulation Graduate!" yard signs to every single high school senior in our area. Of course, high schoolers were cheated out of their last couple months of high school and the yard signs were a great way to celebrate them safely.

Again, Katie activated her massive network and got the word out. The press ran nonstop through the late spring and the yard signs proved to be a blessing to high school students and a much-needed revenue stream for us during those early days of pandemic lockdowns.

* * *

I was 45 when I started my company. My sister Sherrie was 52. I convinced her to leave a good job to join me. She had no experience in printing but had a desire to learn a new profession and industry. We spent two weeks together at a training for new business owners.

Sherrie poured herself into learning. She worked for hours each night to prepare for the next day. After those two weeks, she could operate the machinery; she could operate a small duplicator press, a plate camera, develop film, and make plates. Additionally, and more importantly, she learned the software to estimate jobs, write orders, and create invoices. Knowing I had her efforts and customer service there in the shop, gave me the confidence to keep networking, serving on boards, and selling.

She worked with me for the next seven before retiring. In that time, she never stopped learning. She was another important reason why we stayed in business. I could always count on her. She gets rockstar status too!

* * *

With people like Ernie, Bill, Katie, and Sherrie on my team, I knew the printing company was operating well, so it was my job to make sure we had work coming in. Their excellence pushed me to do my best.

Rockstar employees ask good questions and set a rapid pace of learning. They are curious. They want to know about the financial health of the business, safety issues, new equipment technology, marketing in the digital world, and software releases. They challenge me to keep learning and incorporating their new ideas was essential to our longevity.

While I made many mistakes (as some of my other stories reveal), I never regretted searching for rockstar employees and doing my best to keep them. I made it a top priority to pay well and offer solid benefits and bonuses. I made it a matter of first importance to tell my employees that I appreciate them. Also, I found that employees really appreciated any effort to be flexible on scheduling. Those habits built a very loyal team of people.

Commentary on Reflection 5

The narrative, "Hiring (and stealing) rockstar employees," details how several employees were recruited and hired. In other words, these are accounts of membership negotiation (see Chapter 1). Membership negotiation is paramount among doubting-updating activities in the sense that members are needed to carry on internal constitutive activities. Especially in the context of a new (or small) business, new members share the distributed leadership of the new firm constitution. The emotional tenor of Dee's narratives is sober and grateful. A sense of gravity permeates the reflections as Dee treats recruiting and hiring employees as a serious matter with significant organizational consequences. The stories involve long spans of time. They are about finding employees who are skillful and trustworthy in helping to sustain operations daily, across years—even decades—of employment. Likewise, we detect a sense of gratitude in these accounts as Dee acknowledges the valuable partnership of these members in helping to make her entrepreneurial vision possible and in co-constituting the organization over time. [That gratitude is even more apparent as we read Dee's account of several instances where employees were *not* skillful or trustworthy (see Reflection 6 below)].

The accounts of hiring "rockstar" employees are a matter of membership negotiation. Membership negotiation involves organizational communication that socializes outsider nonmembers into insider-members (and back again). Communicating for membership is so significant that it was identified early in communicative constitution of organizations (CCO) theorizing as a constitutive flow.[15] That observation makes sense because *organization* requires two or more individuals working together. When value propositions are sufficiently complex to require organization (see Chapter 3), members must be recruited, hired, and trained. Without such communication efforts, organization cannot be established. When membership negotiation communication processes are done poorly, organizational constitution will fade and eventually cease to exist.[16–18] Even in established organizations, scholars noted that new members can exert influence on the existing organization—influence that could be positive (e.g., offering new and innovative ideas for work practices) or negative (e.g., a refusal to adopt new and functional practices).[17–19] In other words, it is not that organizations only influence new members; new members influence organization. New members have an especially strong influence in the early days of a new organization because their communication, decisions, and behaviors will set the norms, policies, and practices that form the set point of organization.[20] Thus, membership negotiation communication is especially relevant for understanding new firm creation.

Here, the recruiting, hiring, and training of employees involve doubting-updating activities in a double sense: On one hand, recruiting and hiring a new member implies there is doubt as to whether there are enough current members for the value propositions to be implemented. Of course, there may also be a doubt that current members are skilled enough or skilled in the right ways for the value proposition to be implemented via internal operations. Those doubts trigger updating activities, such as scanning for recruits, networking, asking for referrals, and evaluating applicants, among many others. On the other hand, new members are recruited and hired to engage in doubting-updating activities themselves. When they are especially trustworthy and skillful, their daily interactions and task accomplishments contribute to the doubting-updating activities of organizational constitution.

New members are hired at the outset of organizational constitution to join in constitutive activities. Dee describes the contributions of Ernie, Bill, Katie, and Sherrie as crucial in maintaining internal operations and making the implementation of the printing company's value propositions possible. Additionally, Dee writes with gratitude for their reliable partnership in shouldering the burdens of internal operations, such that she could engage in other relevant constitutive activities. See, for example, how Sherrie's customer service allowed Dee to engage in more networking and sales. Again, these kinds of accounts imply that constitutive leadership is distributed among members and cannot be accomplished by a single entrepreneur.

The accounts also direct our attention to the role played by *ongoing* doubting-updating by "rockstar" employees. For Dee, these best employees have in common a readiness to learn and adapt. Ernie learns new skills, new software, and how to troubleshoot equipment quickly. Bill learns graphic design and how to operate all available machinery. Katie learns the large format printing business and how to leverage her network contacts to grow market demand. Sherrie, despite being close to retirement, learns a new career and all the clerical functions of the company. Individual learning supports the entire organization's learning. It enacts doubting-updating activities, which, taken together, help to constitute the new organization and keep it from becoming unfit with new changes. Individual learning, and its aggregation as organizational learning, implies doubting-updating because to learn implies a starting point of known deficiency (i.e., doubt) in need of remediation through trial-and-error experimentation, advice, or mimicry (i.e., updating). A rich mix of these activities is practiced by Dee's "rockstar" employees.

Likewise, Dee engages in doubting-updating activities in recruitment and hiring. We might ask of Dee's accounts, "How were trustworthy employees identified?" In practical terms, Dee identified them via direct observation (i.e., Ernie), reputation (i.e., Bill), familial association (which is both direct observation and reputation; i.e., Sherrie), and thorough evaluation (i.e., Katie). Each strategy enacts doubting in the sense that individuals were assessed prior to hiring and Dee did not necessarily assume everyone could or would be a beneficial addition to the organization. Research demonstrated that leaders with a reputation for being excellent bosses communicate trust *and* doubt to followers throughout their working relationship.[21] The variety of strategies Dee used for identifying high-quality new employees suggests that no one recruitment strategy is always best, and each situation may need to be met with a new strategy (i.e., updating). Yet, in another sense, these excellent employees were identified by their own patterns of task performance and character across time. Research revealed that leaders use narrative logic to predict members' role performances; narrative reasoning is the way leaders figure out whom they can trust.[20] In other words, leaders take what they know of a member and project that perceived pattern into the future. After all, characters act characteristically. Trust is built or broken in this ongoing personal storytelling of other's characters in the unfolding plotline, which is our work lives. For Dee and these members, the ongoing story was that they are 'rockstars.'

Reflection 6: *A boss's hardest task: Firing employees*
"They did what?!" I shouted.

"Please don't make me say it again," Ernie said, his face flush with embarrassment, staring at the floorboard of my car.

Ernie's car was being repaired and he asked me to drive him to the mechanic on my way home. He hesitated to get out of the car. Finally, he tells me the news I would have never imagined.

"It'll make you mad," he said.

"Please just tell me. I'll keep my cool." Yeah, that didn't happen.

"This afternoon, Victoria and Christopher had sex in the basement bathroom," he mumbled quickly.

Victoria was my office manager and Christopher was one of the Account Representatives for my biggest customer, Pexton and Associates. Our business relationship was so strong that we built our buildings together as a duplex. We even installed a door in the basement between our buildings to make moving back and forth easier. Seems Victoria and Christopher developed a romantic (at least, lusty) relationship and used the common door for their trysts during working hours.

"You know this how?" I asked, looking at him sideways.

"She came into the production office and was bragging about it," said Ernie.

When she arrived the next morning, I motioned for her to come into my office. I instructed her to close the door. She started to remove her coat and I informed her to keep it on.

Told her what I heard. "It that true?" I asked.

"Yes," she confessed.

I told her I was so mad I needed to cool down before I could discuss the consequences of her actions in a professional manner. It was Tuesday morning. I told her to leave and not return until 10 am on Friday. I would let her know if she still had a job. I recommended she explain to her husband why she was sent home.

Then, I went next door to discuss the situation with Jim Pexton, the President of Pexton.

He laughed. I told him I had sent Victoria home and was pretty sure I would be firing her on Friday. I suggested to him that he should do the same with Christopher. I reminded him that Christopher was also married.

A three-day cooling-off period worked well for me over the years. Three days gave me time to think, pray, seek advice, check the employee handbook, and call a human resource attorney. An attorney's hourly rate is cheap compared to a lawsuit. When Victoria returned Friday morning, she was very humble and told me she loved her job and hoped I would keep her. I made my decision to let her go. Trust was lost. I proceeded to tell her that she was terminated and that I did not condone her behavior.

After she left, crying, I went next door to tell Jim what I did. I told him I assumed he would be firing Christopher also. He mumbled around a bit and told me the two of them had decided it was best for Christopher to work from home for a while. That would keep him out of the office and reduce rumors. I was appalled.

* * *

I was looking for a new press operator and Jeremy applied for the job. He was a pleasant-looking man and mild mannered. Jeremy made a very good first impression.

"Before we start our interview, I need to tell you something. I have been an active member of Narcotics Anonymous for about six months. If that is a problem, I understand." Jeremy said.

Jeremy was a drug user, but he was sober for six months. We proceeded with the interview; I observed him operate the press to check his skill and quality. It was excellent. I decided that it was worth a gamble to hire him.

Jeremy was kind and friendly to the staff. He brought his wife and two small children in for us to meet. His productivity was excellent. He became one of the leaders in our local NA organization. All was well for about two years.

One day, two men came in through the backdoor and walked straight toward Jeremy. They held his arms down and proceeded to drag him out the backdoor.

"Hey! I yelled. What's going on? Who do you think you are?" I questioned them out of sheer panic for Jeremy.

"Ma'am, we're Jeremy's NA brothers. He's using again."

I studied Jeremy's reaction. His blank stare told me they were telling the truth.

The men took him to a rehabilitation hospital.

In shock, I called his wife immediately. She knew all about the plan and was thankful for his NA brothers.

He was in the rehabilitation hospital for 30 days. During that time, I sent his paychecks and benefits directly to his wife. When he returned to work, I laid out my expectations in writing. No drugs ever and no absences for the next 90 days. I would be watching his quality and productivity. He agreed and signed the personnel discipline report.

A few weeks later, the same two men arrived again—arm lock and all. He never stopped using and they were once again taking him back to rehab. I stopped them and informed Jeremy that he was fired and that I would send his last paycheck to his wife.

I was disappointed and sad. His betrayal to his wife and children was the hardest to watch.

* * *

Roberta was a friend, whom I hired to be the office manager.

One day, I learned that she lost her job as an office manager for a company that went out of business. Because she was a friend, I assumed I could trust her. I hired her and, among many other tasks, she was responsible for payroll. I made a big mistake and allowed her to sign checks.

After many months, she went on vacation. In her absence, I signed the paychecks.

"Wait. What!?" I said aloud to myself as I studied her paycheck.

Apparently, she decided I was not paying her enough, so she gave herself a substantial raise. Her paycheck was higher than what I paid the top press operator—indicating her arrogance.

Later, I wondered to myself, "Was she responsible for her old company going out of business?"
I called her and fired her. Ugh.
Firing a friend is hard. My emotions ran between disappointment and betrayal. When I let her go, I told her our friendship was over too. Trust was lost. As for me, lesson learned: Sign all your business checks and think twice before hiring a friend.

Commentary on Reflection 6

The autobiographical reflection titled, "A boss's hardest job: Firing employees," offers three counter-examples to reflections on "rockstar" employees presented in Reflection 5. Yet, the counter-examples share a topical consistency with Reflection 5 in that both sets of reflections are about the constitutive consequences of membership negotiation. Also similar to Reflection 5, Dee's accounts of personnel have a particularly emotional element to them. Rather than gratitude (see above), these events have a sense of shock, betrayal, and sadness. Despite negative emotions, the examples of firing employees are no less illustrative of doubting-updating constitutive activities than the more heartening ones of the previous section.

The list of actions that triggered the terminations—sex, drugs, and stealing—read like the lyrics of rock-and-roll song. Here, it is implied that these actions place the employees' continued membership with the organization in jeopardy[21]—in other words, in doubt. Recall that membership negotiation is a matter of doubting and updating constitutive activities in two senses: First, adding (or removing) a member implies a doubt about the fitness of the organization's current membership to deliver its value propositions within the boundaries of material constraints. Second, members themselves often engage in the very doubting-updating activities that keep internal operations going and which co-contribute to organizational constitution. At times, current members' actions (e.g., underperformance or unethical performance) can reveal they are not contributing to organizational constitution through their doubting-updating activities, or that they can no longer be trusted to contribute.

For example, Roberta's decision to pay herself more than was authorized signaled to Dee that Roberta could not be trusted to operate ethically according to the predefined boundaries of her roles, rights, and responsibilities within the organization (i.e., self-structuring communication[15]). Notice how quickly Dee interpreted the discovery as indicating Roberta's presence was not beneficial, but detrimental, to the organization's continued functioning. She then initiated Roberta's termination immediately, and without opportunity for amends, despite being friends. In this sense, Roberta's membership was subject to Dee's doubting-updating activities. More subtly, Roberta's doubting-updating activities no longer co-contributed to organizational constitution, after her termination. Given the severity of the betrayal associated with stealing from the organization's finances, Dee believed that the organization would be better without Roberta's membership. Dee even wonders whether Roberta's presence contributed to the demise of Roberta's previous company. It is especially vital to matters of organizational constitution when doubting-updating activities involve members' handling of materials resources. Material resources can greatly influence whether and when individuals will be perceived as capable of engaging in the organizational constitution or not[22] (see Chapter 1). Careless or unethical uses of the company's finances could quickly undermine perceptions of organizational legitimacy with internal (e.g., employees) and external (e.g., vendors) stakeholders and threaten the existence of the organization.

Across the three examples of terminated employees, one employee is given an opportunity to maintain and rebuild his membership (i.e., Jeremy), while two employees are terminated without that second-chance opportunity (i.e., Victoria and Roberta). In the case of Jeremy's relapse into drug abuse, the drug abuse represented two potentially significant problems for the company: First, poor judgment or slowed reflexes created by drug abuse could create a safety hazard in that press operators manipulate large and dangerous machines, which can and do result in serious bodily harm to self and others.[23] Second, prolonged absences from work, such as with a month-long departure from work to be admitted into rehab, can mean the organization is functioning below its capacity. If the cycle recurred, it could be a serious problem for internal operations and organizational constitution. Ignoring or excusing the drug abuse would have enacted complacency and a lack of adaptation—an approach that could ultimately lead to a deterioration of internal operations and fading organizational constitution (however slowly). Instead, Dee offered Jeremy an opportunity to retain his job with the written agreement that relapse would result in termination. The conversation enacted both doubting and updating in the sense that the agreement communicated some degree of doubt in Jeremy's continued membership and a readiness to update the status of that membership. Indeed, the recurrence of drug abuse was met with the update of membership termination.

In the example of Victoria's extra-marital affair with a client during work hours, we see Dee opts to dismiss Victoria for three days so she can consider whether to terminate her employment. Some scholarship suggests that individuals have two kinds of decisional systems: Broadly speaking, one system involves those effortless, rapid, and intuitive decisions, while the other involves effortful, slower, and calculating decision-making. Of course, optimal decision-making about complex situations likely requires interactions between both of these systems.[24,25] Dee's delaying her decision to terminate Victoria while she deliberated for three days suggests that Dee was moving between these systems. To do so implies a degree of doubt and skepticism in one's immediate and rapid intuition. In fact, Dee seeks the advice of a human resource attorney in those intervening days. Slowing down the decision to seek legal counsel is an example of a doubting-updating activity. Doubting her initial reaction, Dee feared terminating Victoria immediately could have made the company vulnerable to legal action. Those fears were unfounded, and, in this case, her rapid intuition and her slow deliberative process converged such that she moved forward with the termination. Research posited that the entrepreneurs often find themselves needing to make decisions in complex, ambiguous, and rapidly evolving situations with which they may have no prior experiences. In those situations, entrepreneurial *wisdom*—a rich mixture of intuitive (quick) and deliberative (slow) decisions—is needed.[26] Such wisdom implies a readiness to explore the ego-threatening reality that one's first impression could be wrong, that is to doubt and update continually.[27]

Reflection 7: *Lease contracts and other situations when you can't fold*

"The damn thing is down again!" yelled Ernie from the production floor. It was 8:15 am, the day shift just started and the new digital printer was not working again.

"And Sam just left here at five o'clock last night!" I responded. Sam was the technician assigned to our account from our digital printing equipment vendor. He was on site so often that we gave him his own coffee cup and included him in birthday and holiday celebrations.

Digital printing was a new technology and we leased a machine to see how it would complement our offset printing business. When the machine worked, it showed promise as a good investment. That is to say, when *the machine worked.*

My employees eventually just called the digital press, "Lemon."

We had an urgent deadline that morning, so we adjusted and moved the job to an offset press. It was a short-run job. Offset presses are not meant to be used for short runs because they take a lot of setups to start and a lot of clean-up afterward. The adjustment meant we would be losing money on the job.

We leased Lemon 12 months ago. We still had three years left on the lease. Leasing is beneficial in any industry where technology changes fast.

Once it became apparent that the leased equipment could not be fixed, I had several discussions with the sales representative.

"Can you at least trade us for another machine?" I asked.

"We will have Sam take another look at it," was always the response.

We had a year of Lemon and its lease payments. We were looking at three more years of Lemon and lease payments. It seemed like a threat to the life of the business. I finally lost my temper.

"Ernie and Ryan, today I want you to rent a truck and deliver Lemon back to the equipment company. Leave it on their sidewalk for all I care. Just don't come back here with it" I told them. Ernie and Ryan were happy to help.

I called the sales representative and told him where he could find Lemon.

Things got ugly fast. They refused to bring me a new machine without me signing a new lease. I refused to pay the lease payment on Lemon. They sued me for the additional three years.

I hired an attorney and tried mediation. The case eventually went to trial. I hoped a jury would be on our side. However, the fine print on the contract said any litigation would be handled by a judge. The trial took all of two hours and the judge found in favor of my vendor. Lemon cost around $35,000.

With the price of the equipment, interest, court costs, attorney fees, and back payments, I was looking at a $120,000 settlement. We had 36 months to pay it off. In retrospect, I would have been better off moving Lemon into the back corner of the shop and covering it with a blanket.

I wish this story had a happy ending. It did not. It seriously impacted profits for three years and I wasted a lot of time and energy. Now, however, I do count to 100 before I lose my temper. Also, from that day forward, I lived by the lesson: Whoever writes the contract wins.

Commentary on Reflection 7

The reflection, "Lease contracts and other situations when you can't fold," is a cautionary tale about a bad lease deal and a challenging vendor relationship that threatened the existence of a small business. Dee and her employees were exploring a new technology in the printing industry by agreeing to a lease contract. The contract allowed them to acquire and use a digital printing press, which seemed to be (and indeed was) an emerging technology in the industry. On one hand, scanning the environment and testing newly-available technologies are doubting-updating activities that can help keep an organization adapting to new changes.[28] In fact, Dee's company would eventually invest in digital printing and she credits that investment with strengthening the organization and preserving its health to the present day, even after she sold the business (see Chapter 3, Reflection 4). On the other hand, the disadvantageous lease contract combined with the ill-functioning digital press represented a near-catastrophic failure in Dee's doubting-updating activities.

The lease contract kept the small company in a losing position. The fine print of the contract included no stipulation or recourse for the organization to break the lease or get a new press, if it was discovered the equipment was unfixable. In other words, the lease itself denied many possible avenues for updating the disadvantageous situation (at least, from the perspective of the lessee). Over time, the embarrassing nature of the deal became increasingly apparent and painful—a deal that hurt internal operations in terms of financial costs, labor time, and employees' impression of management. The usefulness of the machine is certainly doubted in the story, yet the contract militates against a chance to update the unfavorable vendor relationship.

Dee admits to losing her temper and directs members to deliver the machine back to the vendor, thinking the gesture will get the vendor to take her request for re-negotiation seriously. The move backfires spectacularly and results in severe legal sanctions and financial penalties. In the final analysis, the misstep creates four times the financial harm to the organization as compared to an approach in which the machine was merely ignored, and the lease agreement paid.

The unfolding situation became one of the most severe threats to the organization's existence in 25 years. The lease contract greatly limited members' ability to engage in doubting-updating activities related to digital printing. Fortunately, the organization had other aspects of internal operations in which members could continue doubting-updating activities. On balance and over time, those successes were able to offset losses created by the bad lease deal and subsequent temper-fueled misstep. By way of consolation, Dee comments that the situation taught her a valuable lesson about business contracts and the significant threat they can pose to organizational health and functioning. Thus, the challenging and embarrassing situation is made sense of and somewhat resolved by incorporating the lesson into organizational learning.[29,30]

Reflection 8: *Transforming into a Sustainable Green Printer (SGP)*

"The Board is saying that we should avoid printing to save trees and be more environmentally friendly," my friend told me. My friend was on the board of directors of a local charity. I offered to sponsor one of their events by printing promotional materials for free. She told the board about my offer of free printing. A couple of members responded with their critiques.

"I've heard those comments before," I sighed. "You know, trees are a renewable resource and printing is a recyclable product and can be made from recycled materials. It's one of the better..." I stopped talking, knowing that I just sounded defensive. In some circles, printing had a bad name.

Those lingering criticisms were not uncommon.

Then, the Great Recession of 2008 hit us hard. Customer orders slowed. My employees were nervous. They studied my face and asked questions. Morale tanked. We needed to seize the moment and reinvent ourselves to be ready for when the economy improved.

I'm an avid reader of trade magazines. During those lean years (-2007–2009), I kept reading about the opportunity to go "green," to become more environmentally friendly. I was looking for a way to differentiate us from other printers when the recession ended and going green seemed like a goal that would do it. It might even help address some of those people, like the board members, who considered all printing to be bad for the environment.

As far as I knew, there were no green printers in our area.

About that time, I attended a convention in Indianapolis where a new environmental certification was introduced, called "Sustainable Green Printer" (SGP). SGP is a third-party certification of best practices and innovations that encourage the reduction of environmental harm while increasing corporate social responsibility. The certification process was our path to reinvention. If nothing else, it was a positive distraction and would help us avoid hopelessness and fear, which seemed to be contagious during the Great Recession.

We got the instructional materials. The first step was to create a sustainability committee. I decided my entire staff would be on the committee. We needed complete buy-in and so I wanted everyone to have a voice in decision-making throughout the process. After our first meeting, we agreed we could do all the required physical changes to our plant.

However, the writing of procedures and developing metrics demanded skill and time, which we did not have. The solution was to post an internship position on the University's employment website. Two amazing graduate students applied; we were thrilled. I hired them both. One intern did the procedures and the other handled developing and recording metrics. I agreed to manage the changes needed to bring our physical plant up to the standards of the SGP certification. The process took us a semester before we were ready for the on-site third-party audit. Both interns were present for the eight-hour audit.

That audit was tough. The process involved physical changes in the plant, some grumbling from employees, extensive data collection, mentoring two graduate students, writing and implementing dozens of new procedures and the in-person audit. The process was exhausting and exciting.

We passed the audit; we were certified! At that time, we were the smallest plant in the United States to be certified. From that point forward, we had to get re-certified every two years. I continued to hire graduate student interns to help us prepare for audits.

We transformed our manufacturing processes. Before our green efforts, production in the shop would fill a 30-foot dumpster of waste twice a week. After our green certification, our waste was reduced to a single 65-gallon trash container once a week. Every process had been scrutinized for recycling: paper, plastic, metal, and glass were identified and designated.

Petroleum inks and cleaning solvents were swapped for soy-based inks and non-petroleum cleaning solutions. Large format presses that use harsh chemical toners were swapped with inks that are made of fruits and vegetables.

Big mailer projects used to result in unused paper when mail was undeliverable. To fix the problem, we invested in a postal address verification system and assigned a list manager for our mailing operations. Undeliverable mail was down to just a few pieces a month.

It was not a completely smooth transition. One of my older press operators used petroleum inks and harsh chemical cleaning solutions throughout his career and the change was a challenge for him. Without question, those old materials produce excellent quality and vivid colors. In contrast, soy inks were not as bright and did not lay on the paper as well as petroleum inks. Press operators were adamant that soy cleaning solutions did not get presses clean enough. It was a real dilemma. Dirty presses mean poor-quality printing. I called my ink supplier and made them send an expert to train press operators on the

use of soy ink production. It was still a battle. I think my press opera-
tors taught that expert a few things too. Quality matters.
I decided to purchase a more expensive brand of soy ink and clean-
ing solution. It helped. The press operators knew that they had no
option but to keep working with the soy products; we were not going
back. After two years, the press operators accepted the new products
and were printing materials that they were proud to call their own.
In fact, other plants started calling and asking to get advice from our
operators about how to use soy inks.
By 2010, we were getting attention in the industry; we were the first
of our 900 stores to get certified. I was asked to speak on environmen-
tal sustainability to University classes and on local television news.
Magazine stories were written about us. I was interviewed on a radio
show and asked to speak at service clubs.
Our clients were thrilled to add the SGP logo to their products. A
very large national advertising agency began giving us opportunities
to print for them. They had clients that were asking for the SGP logo
on their products.
We reinvented ourselves as a green printer.

Commentary on Reflection 8

The introduction to the reflection, "Transforming into a Sustainable Green Printer (SGP)," suggests that Dee was aware that there
existed a way of talking and thinking that positioned printing as
illegitimate or unethical because of environmental concerns posed
by the industry. Ways of talking and their related ways of thinking
are called Discourses.[31] Whether Dee was fully aware of it or not,
the pro-environment/anti-print Discourse she encountered represented a threat to the company and industry. Imagine a scenario in
which the perception (whether accurately or inaccurately) grew that
printing was an outdated and even unethical approach to business,
advertising, branding, and public messaging. Printing is sometimes
positioned as pollution and vilified in some circles.[32,33] If that sentiment grew and was widely shared, potential customers would
want to distance themselves from these negative associations and
find better alternatives. Thus, Discourses can represent existential
challenges to organizations. Indeed, public sentiment shapes and is
shaped by Discourses, which can, in turn, interact with organizational constitution in complex ways.[34,35]

After hearing the anti-print Discourse periodically, Dee gathered
some communication strategies for defending the industry's image

and her own company's image by extension. The lull in workflow during the recession, however, created an opportunity in which the lack of work and a need to address the Discourse came together. Scholarship demonstrated that specific industrial practices in the printing industry, such as those involving the use of volatile organic compounds and heavy metals, are harmful to the environment but opting for environmentally friendly alternatives can reduce these harms.[36] In fact, one study revealed that where printing companies operate in rapidly changing markets and have a habit of innovation, they are more likely to adopt environmentally friendly printing practices.[37] Dee's company is an example of that finding. Also, communication research demonstrated that management can often internalize the rhetoric of their own defense of products, which can, in turn, keep them from making needed changes and avoiding crisis and decline.[27,38] Dee and her employees avoided that trap through doubting-updating activities. They engaged in extensive improvements and upgrades to their internal operations to align with green printing practices. In doing so, they prepared a resource to reshape and defend the credibility and legitimacy of their product and organizational image with stakeholders (i.e., institutional positioning).

The narrative includes many doubting-updating activities. First, Dee's willingness to even consider the pro-environmental/anti-print Discourse and avoid defensiveness is an example of her doubting her company's position. Significant ego defense mechanisms,[27] such as denial and displacement, were likely motivating Dee and employees to avoid consideration of the environmental critique because to accept it would imply the need for significant changes. Despite that challenge, Dee and her employees did not fall prey to overconfidence but engaged in an honest doubting of their operations, collectively and democratically. Within the narrative, we also see a press operator doubting whether the soy-based inks were of sufficient quality. That doubt eventually led to yet another update to more expensive, although still environmentally-friendly, soy-based inks such that production quality was maintained. Updating activities undertaken by every employee (including graduate interns!) were numerous and resulted in massive changes in internal operations. The doubting-updating efforts created shifts in equipment, procedures, products, and waste management. By the end, the company earned a new certification, which bolstered its legitimacy with stakeholders. Here, the relationship between the doubting-updating activities that constitute internal operations and the legitimizing-multiplying activities that constitute external organizational image overlap and influence one another reciprocally. Chapter 5 describes legitimizing-multiplying/sustaining activities in greater detail.

Conclusion

This chapter described the second set of entrepreneurial activities in the SEA model, which involve the constitution of internal operations. Doubting and updating activities are needed to adjust internal operations ongoingly so that the value propositions which motivate the need for an organization can be implemented. The autobiographical reflections offered in this chapter point to the diverse ways that doubting-updating activities are distributed across members and over time. Without doubting-updating activities, the organization itself fades definitionally or can decline systemically and can even cease to exist if critical matters are ignored for too long enough. The following chapter describes the final set of entrepreneurial activities for organizational constitution, legitimizing-multiplying/sustaining.

Notes

1 Weick, K. E. (1974). Middle range theories of social systems. *Behavioral Science, 19*(6), 357–367.
2 Weick, K. E., & Sutcliffe, K. M. (2006). Mindfulness and the quality of organizational attention. *Organization Science, 17*(4), 514–524. doi:10.1287/orsc.1060.0196.
3 Weick, K. E., & Westley, F. (1999). Organizational learning: Affirming an oxymoron. In S. R. Clegg, C. Hardy, & W. R. Nord (Eds.), *Managing organizations: Current issues* (pp. 190–208). Thousand Oaks, CA: Sage.
4 Rice, R. E. (2008). Unusual routines: Organizational (non)sensemaking. *Journal of Communication, 58*(1), 1–19. doi:10.1111/j.1460-2466.2007. 00371.x.
5 Langer, E. J. (1989). *Mindfulness.* Boston, MA: Addison-Wesley.
6 Maitlis, S., & Sonenshein, S. (2010). Sensemaking in crisis and change: Inspiration and insights from Weick (1988). *Journal of Management Studies, 47*(3), 551–580. doi:10.1111/j.1467–6486.2010.00908.x.
7 Burgoon, J. K., & Langer, E. J. (1995). Language, fallacies, and mindlessness-mindfulness in social interaction. *Annals of the International Communication Association, 18*(1), 105–132.
8 Weick, K. E., & Sutcliffe, K. M. (2011). *Managing the unexpected: Resilient performance in an age of uncertainty.* New York: John Wiley & Sons.
9 Weick, K. E., Sutcliffe, K. M., & Obstfeld, D. (2005). Organizing and the process of sensemaking. *Organization Science, 16*(4), 409–421. doi:10.1287/orsc.1050.0133.

10　Weick, K. E., & Sutcliffe, K. M. (2003). Hospitals as cultures of entrapment: A re-analysis of the Bristol Royal Infirmary. *California Management Review, 45*(2), 73–84.
11　Simon, H. A. (1972). Theories of bounded rationality. *Decision and Organization, 1*(1), 161–176.
12　Simon, H. A. (1991). Bounded rationality and organizational learning. *Organization Science, 2*(1), 125–134.
13　Bisel, R. S., Fairhurst, G. T., & Sheep, M. L. (2022). CCO theory and leadership. In J. Basque, N. Bencherki, & T. Kuhn (Eds.), *Routledge handbook of CCO* (pp. 297–309). New York: Routledge.
14　Burkus, D. (2013). *The myths of creativity: The truth about how innovative companies and people generate great ideas.* San Francisco, CA: John Wiley & Sons.
15　McPhee, R. D., & Zaug, P. (2000). The communicative constitution of organizations: A framework for explanation. *Electronic Journal of Communication, 10*(1 and 2), 1–16.
16　Scott, C. W., & Myers, K. K. (2010). Toward an integrative theoretical perspective of membership negotiations: Socialization, assimilation, and the duality of structure. *Communication Theory, 20*, 79–105. doi:10.1111/j.1468–2885.2009.01355.x.
17　Kramer, M. W. (2011). Toward a communication model for the socialization of voluntary members. *Communication Monographs, 78*(2), 233–255. doi:10.1080/03637751.2011.564640.
18　Endacott, C. G., & Myers, K. K. (2019). Extending the membership negotiation model: Previous work experience and the reproduction and transformation of structures. *Management Communication Quarterly, 33*(4), 455–483. doi:10.1177/08933189861555.
19　Lutgen-Sandvik, P., & McDermott, V. (2008). The constitution of employee-abusive organizations: A communication flows theory. *Communication Theory, 18*(2), 304–333. doi:10.1111/j.1468-2885.2008.00324.x.
20　Giddens, A. (1984). *The constitution of society.* Oakland, CA: University of California Press.
21　Kelley, K. M., & Bisel, R. S. (2014). Leaders' narrative sensemaking during LMX role negotiations: Explaining how leaders make sense of who to trust and when. *The Leadership Quarterly, 25*(3), 433–448. doi:10.1016/j.leaqua.2013.10.011.
22　Bruscella, J. S., & Bisel, R. S. (2018). Four flows theory and materiality: ISIL's use of material resources in its communicative constitution. *Communication Monographs, 85*(3), 331–356. doi:10.1080/03637751.2017.1420907.
23　United States Department of Labor Occupational Health and Safety Administration (OSHA). (2022). *Printing industry: Health and safety concerns.* Retrieved from https://www.osha.gov/printing-industry/health-safety-concerns.
24　Kahneman, D. (2011). *Thinking, fast and slow.* New York: Macmillan.
25　Milkman, K. L., Chugh, D., & Bazerman, M. H. (2009). How can decision making be improved?. *Perspectives on Psychological Science, 4*(4), 379–383. doi:10.1111/j.1745-6924.2009.01142.x.
26　Dunham, L., McVea, J., & Freeman, R. E. (2008). Entrepreneurial wisdom: Incorporating the ethical and strategic dimensions of

entrepreneurial decision-making. *International Journal of Entrepreneurship and Small Business, 6*(1), 8–19.

27 Brown, A. D., & Starkey, K. (2000). Organizational identity and learning: A psychodynamic perspective. *Academy of Management Review, 25*(1), 102–120.

28 Bushnell, M. (2022). Equipment leasing: A guide for business owners. *Business News Daily.* Retrieved from https://www.businessnewsdaily. com/8083-equipment-leasing-guide.html.

29 Heinze, I. (2013). Entrepreneur sense-making of business failure. *Small Enterprise Research, 20,* 21–39. doi:10.5172/ser.2013.20.1.21.

30 Alvarado Valenzuela, J. F., Wakkee, I., Martens, J., & Grijsbach, P. (2020). Lessons from entrepreneurial failure through vicarious learning. *Journal of Small Business & Entrepreneurship,* 1–25. doi:10.108 0/08276331.2020.1831839.

31 Jian, G., Schmisseur, A. M., & Fairhurst, G. T. (2008). Organizational discourse and communication: The progeny of Proteus. *Discourse & Communication, 2*(3), 299–320. doi:10.1177/1750481308091912.

32 See for example: Sarwar, M. Z. (2021, February 3). Is printing bad for the environment? *Techengage.* Retrieved from https://techengage. com/is-printing-bad-for-the-environment.

33 See a parallel debate around newspaper printing described here: Zeller, T. Jr. (2009, April 19). Skip the newspaper, save the planet? *The New York Times.* Retrieved from https://www.nytimes.com/2009/04/20/ technology/20green.html.

34 Kuhn, T. (1997). The discourse of issues management: A genre of organizational communication. *Communication Quarterly, 45*(3), 188–210.

35 Fairhurst, G. T., & Putnam, L. (2004). Organizations as discursive constructions. *Communication Theory, 14*(1), 5–26. doi:10.1111/j.1468-2885.2004.tb00301.x.

36 Aydemir, C., & Özsoy, S. A. (2020). Environmental impact of printing inks and printing process. *Journal of Graphic Engineering and Design, 11*(2), 11–17. doi:10.24867/JGED-2020–2–011.

37 Rothenberg, S., & Zyglidopoulos, S. C. (2007). Determinants of environmental innovation adoption in the printing industry: The importance of task environment. *Business Strategy and the Environment, 16*(1), 39–49. doi:10.1002/bse.441.

38 Heath, R. L. (1990). Effects of internal rhetoric on management response to external issues: How corporate culture failed the asbestos industry. *Journal of Applied Communication Research, 18*(2), 153–167.

5 Legitimizing-Multiplying/Sustaining Entrepreneurial Activities of New Organizational Constitution

Abstract

Gaining recognition from important stakeholders, such as customers, vendors, and government agencies, is crucial to establishing and maintaining a new organization. The task of getting positive credibility with stakeholders is at the heart of one of the many puzzles of entrepreneurship and organizational constitution. In the present chapter, entrepreneurial activities involving *external* stakeholders (i.e., legitimizing-multiplying/sustaining) are discussed. Perhaps you have heard the saying, "Your career is in other people's hands[1]"? This section offers the parallel observation that organizational constitution is (at least partially) in the hands of external stakeholders. Without question, external stakeholders are incredibly important in whether a new organization survives and thrives. That realization raises the question: "How do we get outsiders to treat us and our vision *as a legitimate organization*?" In everyday life, it is easy to forget that every retail store, service provider company, or church was once the idea of one or a few individuals. When we shop at Macy's, file our taxes with H&R Block, or attend a worship service in a grand chapel, it can be easy to ignore that such seemingly permanent organizations were once fuzzy entrepreneurial visions that required new organizational constitution. They seem so stable, so finished. Yet, the main idea of this book is to redirect attention upstream to the origins and maintenance of all organizations from within fleeting and flowing communication.

As the owner of a printing company, Dee interacted at the front desk with dozens of would-be entrepreneurs who were attempting to choose their business cards, logos, and letterhead. The experience was painful for Dee, at times. Would-be business owners would agonize over the $30 purchase of business cards. (Sheesh!). Yet, they agonized—knowingly or unknowingly—because they had the sense

DOI: 10.4324/9781003291312-5

that the humble 3- by 2-inch cardstock was genuinely important to their constitutive efforts. That is to say that the simple card was a part of a communication strategy to get others to believe that the business owner was more than an individual—he or she represented an organization. These would-be entrepreneurs would often add the phrase "& Associates," "Group," or other official-sounding labels to their business names. With a whisper and a wink, the would-be entrepreneur would say, "People will never know it's really just me!" Such encounters were so common they became the butt of inside jokes among Dee's printing company employees. Few of these would-be entrepreneurs would go on to establish organizations that survived over the long term. Yet, the fact remains that many intuited that the symbolism of a company name and business card was more than a "mere" $30 purchase. Whether they could state it so plainly or not, they knew communication mattered to being seen as a legitimate organization by customers, clients, and vendors.

In this chapter, we describe the Legitimizing and Multiplying/ Sustaining interplay in greater detail by leveraging Dee's autobiographical reflections on owning a business and attempting to get key external stakeholders to recognize her printing company *as a legitimate organization*. As with Chapters 3 and 4, it is somewhat inappropriate to discuss any one set of activities without discussing the other sets simultaneously because each of these sets of entrepreneurial activities feeds forward and backward to the others. However, the opportunity to focus on legitimizing-multiplying/sustaining activities and their interplay will provide conceptual clarity and an opportunity to illustrate the point more fully.

Autobiographical Reflections of Legitimizing-Multiplying/Sustaining

Reflection 9: *"Your husband really runs the company, right?": Certifying as a Women's Business Enterprise*

"Dammit it! Not again!" I threw the letter on my desk and sank into my chair.

For the third time in three years, I was rejected by the State of Kansas, Department of Commerce, Office of Minority and Women Business Development. The agency declined again to certify me as a Women's Business Enterprise (WBE). Why?: My business was deemed a franchise—a label that excluded me from the government certification.

I had been in business for three years before I applied for the first time. So there I was, six years in business, and still not certified. The

WBE certification held the possibility of getting more government work—and government dollars—flowing through the company. The application was 15 pages of legalese and required a dozen different documents, such as profit and loss reports, balance sheets, and tax returns. Answering bureaucratic forms and rounding up the documents involved days of tiring work.

Weeks later I attended a Chamber of Commerce event. Representative Barbara Ballard of Kansas happened to be at the event. I saw my moment.

Introducing myself, I told Barbara my story. As she listened, I could see that my struggles with achieving WBE status surprised her. Her frown suggested she was as irritated as I was—I found an ally, and a powerful one at that. After some kind words of consolation from Barbara, we parted ways.

Two weeks passed when I received a letter from the Office of Minority and Women Business Development. Seems Barbara had made a visit to the department on my behalf. They informed me they would be doing an in-person interview with me at my production plant. That was further in the process than I have ever got on my own! I was thrilled. Perhaps, a little prematurely.

A week later, two women, Cathy and Karen, arrived at the plant. Their demeanor made it obvious that neither one wanted to be there. A long day of questioning unfolded, which made it clear that they were intent on proving my franchise agreement meant that either I was a puppet of the franchise or that my husband really ran the business. My job was to convince them that neither of their assumptions was correct. They sat down at my desk and asked if they could record our conversation. I agreed. A six-hour marathon of interrogation began.

After a few hours, the investigators asked to interview my employees, I readily agreed and made a quick announcement to my employees to answer any of their questions. At the conclusion of the day, my employees were eager to share.

They told me they were asked questions, such as:
"How often does her husband come into the building?"
"Who hired you?"
"Who does the firing?"
My employees only see my husband at our annual Christmas party; I hired them and I handle all firing. Additionally, the investigators asked my accountant to pull all the checks for the last two years. One by one, they verified that I signed all the checks—not my husband. They were especially interested in payroll checks and purchase orders. They also confirmed that I signed all checks for the past two years, including

payroll checks and checks to vendors. They could find no evidence of franchise influence or that my husband ever worked in the business.

Interrogations reconvened after lunch. More hours passed. Admittedly, I was getting tired and irritated at the thought that these female investigators could not imagine I, a woman, was the true business owner and operator.

Then I got an idea: I asked the ladies, "Please turn off the tape recorder for a minute." Gesturing to the production floor, I asked them to look at the large copier outside my office. "I plan to go out there and open the top of the copier, drop my pants, hop up on the copier and prove to you that I'm a woman!" I slid my chair back and stood.

As I took a step toward the door, Cathy asked me to stop. They agreed to complete the last 15 minutes of the interview and be on their way.

A month later I received my Women's Business Enterprise (WBE) certification in the mail. To my surprise, there was also a Disadvantaged Business Enterprise (DBE) certification included. Turns out, I also qualified for that designation. So, I now had two certifications in the eyes of the government, in addition to a Small Business status.

Representative Ballard called me the following week to congratulate me and let me know that the State had removed the "No Franchise" clause in their requirements. I thanked her for her help and told her she would be getting my vote for as long as she wanted to be my Representative.

Three years later, I received a phone call from a large government subcontractor. They were looking for a vendor in the area to print training manuals for their call center—a massive facility that handles Medicare and Medicaid questions throughout the Midwest.

Steve, a buyer, saw our advertisement in the phone book, which included, in small letters, "Woman Owned Business." He asked about that point specifically.

"Yes, I am certified by the State, also a DBE and yes, a small business," I responded.

He laughed and said, "Well, I just hit the trifecta!"

He told me that as a government subcontractor he could report to the government three times for every dollar he spent with us. For example, if he spent $100,000 with us he could report $100,000 under WBE, $100,000 under DBE, and $100,000 under Small Business. We got the contract and developed a wonderful working relationship.

Steve was promoted to their Washington DC office and called me one day to see if I would consider quoting on printing the training manuals for the entire country. I came up with a plan to use other franchise plants across the country to do the production and delivery to the Medicare and Medicaid plants near them. We would produce for the Lawrence facility. We would be the sole contractor and handle all the paperwork and communication with our sister franchise plants and our client. We got the national contract. Later, we got the Afford-able Care Act contract too for much the same reasons. That was 15 years ago, and we still have the contract.

Furthermore, after we received certification, the State University closed its own printing facility. This was a tremendous opportunity for all the local printing companies: We were the only WBE and DBE print-ing companies listed on the State Department of Commerce website. We used it to our advantage by telling all our University connections about our new certifications. Soon, we were printing for many Univer-sity Departments that had the government and corporate grants, which encouraged the use of WBE or DBE subcontractors. The certifications opened many doors to growth opportunities—many of which I could not have imagined when I started. So, yes, the struggle was worth it!

Commentary on Reflection 9

The autobiographical reflection, "'Your husband really runs the company, right?': Certifying as a Women's Business Enterprise" is a tale about the challenges of interacting with state government as a key external stakeholder. Recall the fourth premise from the four flows model states that both internal and external message flows matter to organizational constitution.[2–4] A main idea of the SEA model is that creating and maintaining an organization requires a lot of things to go well. Neglecting internal operations for the sake of sales can be as dangerous to organizational survival as is neglect-ing sales for the sake of operations. Dee's reflection illustrates that several activities were needed in her ongoing organizational main-tenance efforts; the story is about how the effort to get recognized by external stakeholders was difficult, but well worth it, in terms of its payoff for her company's longevity.

Dee's company was helped significantly by her success at con-vincing Representative Ballard, and the state investigators, that she deserved the WBE designation. The certification eventually meant contracts and contracts meant a steady stream of work and money. Here, the legitimizing-multiplying interplay is obvious. Achieving success in obtaining her company's rightful identification with the Office of Minority and Women Business Development allowed her company greater ability to be recognized as a legitimate organization with still other organizations and desirable external stakeholders. In this case, the state government certifications were strong legitimizing credibility with a government subcontractor buyer. One external stakeholder (a state government agency) was essentially vouching for the legitimacy of Dee's company to another external stakeholder (a government subcontractor and potential client). Dee's legitimizing activities were connected to multiplying activities in the sense that gaining certifications (legitimizing) created possibilities for rapid growth (multiplying) that would not have been likely otherwise.

What about the troubling challenge Dee faced in getting the female investigators to believe she was the rightful business owner— and not her husband? Unfortunately, research suggests that women tend to be viewed as less capable or less likely to be entrepreneurs than their male counterparts.[5] However, research demonstrated that women entrepreneurs can and do resist cultural stereotypes in creative and forceful ways,[6,7] as we see with Dee's (*ahem*) ultimatum to auditors. The creative tactic helped Dee move the conversation forward productively in her favor and earn the certification and its legitimizing consequences.

What do widespread culturally gendered stereotypes mean for organizational constitution? Written plainly, gendered stereotypes point to the (unfortunate!) reality that not all individuals will find it equally easy to create organizations. Consider these two points: (a) being seen as a legitimate organization by stakeholders is important for organizational constitution, and (b) those stakeholders are biased. Therefore, not all individuals have an equal shot at being successful in organizational constitution (see the unequal constitutive capacity addendum[8] described in Chapter 1). In other words, resources—such as money and even cultural assumptions—should not be underestimated in terms of their ability to help or hurt entrepreneurs convince external stakeholders of the legitimacy of their constitutive efforts.

How, then, did Dee overcome her apparent constitutive disadvantage in this regard? Three lessons stand out: First, notice how a single powerful ally created momentum where none could be generated previously. Dee's applications were rejected three times, three years in a row. Completing the tedious bureaucratic paperwork was increasingly frustrating. Yet, a turning point of the reflection involves the chance encounter with Representative Ballard, which presented a communication opportunity: Dee shared her struggles with the congresswoman, who was concerned about the situation enough to get involved on Dee's behalf. The congresswoman was a powerful ally in Dee's legitimizing activities. The congresswoman used her political capital and power on Dee's behalf with the certifying agency. Representative Ballard's advocacy helped Dee's application get noticed and taken seriously. However, enlisting a powerful ally was only a part of the legitimizing activities. The story gives us the impression that the congresswoman's advocacy created forward progress; however, that progress was not without consequences. The state investigators seemed to approach the site visit with the mindset of *in*validating the application.

Second, the reflection suggests that document evidence was important to Dee's legitimizing activities. A powerful political ally was helpful, but the historical evidence provided by copious documentation (e.g., payroll checks) and firsthand witnesses (e.g., employees' testimony) were crucial in this situation for achieving success. If documentation is the coin of the bureaucratic realm,[9] then Dee was able to supply the government investigators with gold bullion. These artifacts serve a powerful legitimizing function in the eyes of an important external stakeholder (i.e., the Department of Commerce). At this point, the story suggests that the combination of an ally and documentation was helpful but not entirely conclusive in convincing the investigators that their plans to invalidate the application were wrong. The reflection's final tipping point was triggered by Dee's confidence and boldness. Dee showed strong negative emotion in giving the investigators an aggressive (although humorous) ultimatum. The third lesson here is that well-timed displays of confidence and boldness are also legitimizing activities. In this case, a powerful ally, copious documentation, and confidence were legitimizing activities that won the day, despite her disadvantage as a woman business owner. The reality of unequal constitutive capacity is unfair; however, this account provides insight into the ways individuals work communicatively to overcome unfair reality.

Reflection 10: *Paying your dues is not enough*
"I'll be back in a little while. I'm walking down to the Chamber of Commerce office to join." I called to Sherrie, as I headed out the door of the shop. It was our second day in business. Sherrie was my sister. She decided to leave her job and join me on my entrepreneurial adventure. Our husbands were skeptical of us working together, but it was a great arrangement. Her dedication to customer service, estimating, order writing, and production made it possible for me to build the company's visibility. I immersed myself in the community. The plan was for me to get involved in the community. We reasoned visibility would lead to sales. Every entrepreneur needs a Sherrie.

I began by attending a local Chamber event. There, I met Barbara, who was eager to get me participating.

"Have you considered being a member of the Envoy Committee?" Barbara asked. "The committee is super active. They attend all the ribbon cuttings for new businesses in town. Seems like a good place to see and be seen, don't you think?"

"Well, yes it does! Sign me up." I replied grateful for the advice and nudge.

After a year of serving on the committee, I was asked to be chair. Sixty-one ribbon cuttings would happen that year. The envoy committee work provided a convenient excuse to get an introduction. I visited each entrepreneur and new owner and left them with my business card and gifts of memo pads and pens with my company's logo. When their ribbon-cutting day arrived, I included personal anecdotes from the owner that I discovered on my visit. By year's end, I had 61 new customers. Every. Single. One.

The following year I was asked to sit on the Chamber Board of Directors. From there I was asked to serve on the Boards of United Way, SERTOMA, Junior Achievement, Meals on Wheels, and other nonprofits. Board positions give you the opportunity to meet and work with the owners, CEO's and Presidents of all the local businesses. It is a great opportunity and responsibility. I accepted leadership positions. The friendships that resulted from working and volunteering were rewarding, fun, and very good for business. When the CEO of a company tells a purchasing agent to "Call Dee for this printing project," we gain a new longtime client, who rarely asks the price!

As a Chamber Board member, I helped to sell new memberships. I often heard the objection, "I joined the Chamber years ago, but they never got me any business, so I stopped paying my dues."

That is not how it works. Just like anything in life—you get out of it what you put into it. Simply paying membership dues won't equate to new customers. It takes time and commitment. Volunteer to be on committees, take a leadership position, attend events, and take a sincere interest in other members and their businesses.

My friend, Jeanie, was the interim President of the Chamber while the Board recruited a new leader. The Chamber and the city's Economic Development team recruited a large machinery manufacturing company to town. They were Chamber members for a couple of years. Then they stopped paying their dues. Jeanie visited the plant, talked to the CEO, and asked why they had dropped their membership? She recounts that he yelled at her and told her that it was the Chamber's fault they were about to close because they (the Chamber) did not help him recruit good employees. She was shocked and asked him when he had asked for help recruiting. He admitted he had not asked for help. They closed the following summer.

Business referral groups are a great way of adding new business and developing new friendships. Referral groups are usually made up of entrepreneurs and new business owners who help one another get new clients. I participated in one for 20 years; we organized and managed it ourselves and so the cost was minimal. In referral groups, the objective is to give at least one referral or "lead" to another club member each week. For instance, fellow referral group members, Wilson Lawn and Landscape, mow my lawn. My neighbor compliments my lawn and asks who I use. The following week I give my neighbor's contact information to Wilson Lawn and Landscape for this week's lead. Also, members are expected to do business with each other. New members must be nominated by a current member. Only one person from each broad commercial category (e.g., accounting, banking, and plumbing) is allowed to join. I highly recommend joining or starting a referral group.

Your business circle should include a least one mentor. One of my early Chamber friends, Sheryl owned an employment firm; she was a former mayor and an all-around smart businesswoman. During my company's early years, Sheryl answered my questions patiently. She advised me on which nonprofits had the best reputations and encouraged me to get involved. She introduced me to many other business leaders. She gave great advice about personnel issues, and I used her firm.

As I look back over my years in business, it is apparent to me that my best friendships have a link to the Chamber. Remember Barbara who signed me up? Her husband, Bill had a poker game at their house every Thursday night. Barbara got tired of cooking for the guys. So, she suggested that two other acquaintances, Sonya, Teri, and I go shopping one Thursday evening. I did not know Sonya or Teri prior to our shopping trip. We shopped for about a half hour and then ended up in a local sports bar. That was the beginning of a support group that lasted 25 years. We met every Thursday night for drinks and conversation. We called ourselves the Thursday Pub Club (TPC).

The four of us became each other's inner circle. TPC was our safe space to share our business challenges, personnel issues, financial needs, family celebrations, heartaches, and personal problems. We traveled together at least twice a year. Their support and advice were priceless.

The Chamber might not be the business hub in your town. It might be by the Rotary Club or other civic organizations. Identify that organization and get involved.

Commentary on Reflection 10

The autobiographical reflection, "Paying your dues is not enough" is a narrative about the effort needed to network successfully on behalf of a new company. Within the narrative, Dee seeks to access the network of legitimate entrepreneurs and business owners in the city via association with the Chamber of Commerce. The efforts are foreshadowed by a mention of Sherrie, the member whose efforts at maintaining internal operations (through doubting-updating, see Chapter 4) make Dee's external entrepreneurial efforts possible— a reminder that constitutive leadership is often distributed among many members.[10]

As for networking, imagine the web of relationships that exist in any city among businesses and their representatives. That network is of great social value for entrepreneurial efforts at organizational constitution in that stakeholders *who know* others in the network and *are known by* others in the network *are in the know* with regard to valuable insights and resources.[11] For the representatives and organizations to know and be known by key stakeholders in the network is to garner critical perceptions of legitimacy for a new organization. However, we see that the tale is cautionary in that mere membership with the Chamber association is "not enough" to generate perceptions of legitimacy and the in-flow of resources from the network. Instead, the reflection emphasizes the need for a social and relational *presence* in conversations with other members in an ongoing manner. Recall that institutional positioning is a constitutive communication flow of organizations (see Chapter 1). Institutional positioning refers to communication in which the organization is presented as an organization to key external stakeholders.[2] Institutional positioning becomes an important activity through which new organizations get resources, vendors, and customers.[3,11] Dee's social and relational presence at Chamber functions and her dialoguing with other members in the first year of her organizational constitution efforts served to present her new company as an organization.

At ribbon-cutting ceremonies, she represented the Chamber as an organization and her new company as an organization to other representatives of still other new organizations. Together, the mix of interactions among entrepreneurs and organizational members was making new organizations "present" via their re-*present*-atives.[12–14] In this way, we can see the opportunity to accept a position with the envoy committee is a legitimizing activity, but also a multiplying activity. The question from Barbara appears to be advice in that it nudged Dee toward the advantageous role of the envoy committee chair. A single interaction with a new business owner via cold call could be helpful. In contrast, accepting the envoy committee role multiplied the potential for interactions with new business owners and members and did so alongside the helpful credibility and legitimacy afforded by her role with the Chamber. The net result of new customers that year demonstrates the success of the entrepreneurial efforts of legitimizing-multiplying.

The committee work allowed Dee to inhabit a legitimized role with the Chamber. She communicated on behalf of the Chamber with others as a representative. That role likely helped to close the open question of her own organization's existence and legitimacy in the minds of many in the network of stakeholders. She passed out business cards, memo pads, and pens to individuals who were attempting to constitute their own organizations. From the vantage point of the new business owner, Dee's company's existence would have seemed an incontestable and taken-for-granted reality. At the end of her retrospective account, Dee can identify still more connections that would ultimately be helpful to her constitutional efforts, which stemmed from the association with the Chamber. Networking begets networking.[15]

Reflection 11: *You can't take it off your taxes: Our charitable donations policy*

"Ding!" The front door rang to indicate a customer was walking into the shop.

"Hello. I'm Maxine," said a woman, who held out her hand for a handshake. I recognized her as a community leader. "I'm the volunteer chairperson this year for the county fair," she said smiling.

Being new to town and new in business, I knew nothing about the event, but I was pleased to have a potential customer.

She proceeded to tell me that she was giving us the "honor" of printing the program for the county rodeo. My excitement around selling a job was soon squashed as she proceeded, "Of course, it would be a donation. But we could put an ad in the program at no cost to you." She concluded her pitch by reassuring me, "Your donation is tax deductible."

"Okay. Can you give me more details on the program? What are its specs?" I asked.

"Oh, just a few pages. And we'll need a few hundred copies," she said.

My ego got the best of me that day, and I agreed without pressing for more information. The conversation occurred in May. The county fair and rodeo were in late July. Plenty of time. By mid-June, I pressed Maxine for more details and page copy. The plan was for my employees to complete the charity work while we were slow in-between paying jobs. That did not happen.

By July, I kept telling myself it was no big deal, "Only a few copies, right?"

Two weeks before the rodeo, Maxine walked into the shop with a pile of papers. Each page was from a separate sponsor. The papers were a haphazard mix of handwritten notes; nothing was camera ready. I panicked.

The next two weeks were hell. I hired a graphic designer to produce the 16 pages of camera-ready artwork. The job could not be copied. It had to be printed on our offset presses because of the length of the runs, which meant the work was expensive to produce. She needed 4,000, 16-page programs; it was an $8,000 job—an amount that exceeded how much work we had sold since we opened! Here we were, doing it for free.

My small staff worked day and night and weekends. We purchased graphic design; we made negatives and metal plates; we purchased paper. Presses ran constantly. We did the time-consuming and laborious tasks of folding, collating, and stapling—all with the painful realization that we would not see a payment. The program was delivered a mere two hours before the rodeo started.

As a thank you, Maxine arranged for me and my family plus my employees and their families to ride in the rodeo parade. As our horse-drawn wagon passed the VIP section, where Maxine was sitting, we gave her the single-finger salute. Not my finest moment, but what can I say? We felt duped.

Monday morning my employees and I sat down to discuss (and just cuss) the rodeo program and our situation. My foolishness had put our company in financial jeopardy. After we all voiced our frustrations, I asked, "How do we handle contribution requests in the future?" After a couple of hours of discussion, we crafted a contribution policy together. We wanted to be charitable, but we wanted to stay in business too. The following is the policy that guided us for 29 years.

CHARITABLE CONTRIBUTION POLICY:

[Our company] will make one printing contribution per month. We require a written letter requesting the contribution with timeframe and complete job details. Any organization requesting the contribution must show proof of non-for-profit status, that is, 501(c)(3). Maximum contribution will be 50% of the retail value of the job or $500 (whichever is smallest). The

organization will permit [the company] to add an acknowledg-
ment on the printed piece or receive a free advertisement. A
50% down payment will be required on the day [we] received
the copy with the balance due on the day of delivery or pick-up.

*Contributions were made on a first-come, first-served basis, which
kept us from having to decline worthy requests. Instead, we showed
requestors the policy and encouraged them to plan to participate in
the upcoming month. The policy—and our company's generosity—
benefitted from a lot of word-of-mouth in the community and among
nonprofits. Within a few years, all 12 months would be assigned by
mid-January. Nonprofits learned fast and were eager to benefit. Over
the years, I have been surprised by how many non-profit directors and
their board members know about the policy and thank me. The public
relations and personal satisfaction that has come from working with
the non-profits have been wonderful.*

*When I was preparing for my first year's taxes, I remember what
Maxine told me. So, I listed my $8,000 loss, which I provided to my
accountant. He called me and informed me that only cash contributions to a 501(c)(3) could be deducted. Not "in-kind contributions"
of material services. Furthermore, I learned the county fair was not
a 501(c)(3). So, no you can't take it off your taxes. Do it because it's
the right thing to do.*

Another expensive lesson learned.

Commentary on Reflection 11

"You can't take it off your taxes: Our charitable contributions policy"
is a reflection on an early mistake that threatened the existence of a
new company. Organizational constitution is precarious at the outset of entrepreneurial activities; stories such as these draw our attention to perils hiding in innocuous places for the establishment of new
firms. But what causes the mistake of promising an in-kind contribution to the county fair without a full understanding of the request? It
seems that Dee understood intuitively the charitable contribution was
an opportunity to engage in legitimizing activities. It is remarkable
that Dee describes the error as created by her ego—a humble con-
fession. Read from the perspective of the SEA model, we see that the
mistake was likely motivated by an intuition that she needed to seize
upon opportunities to legitimize the new organization's existence in
the minds of important stakeholders. Maxine was a community leader
and representative of the county fair; therefore, Dee saw her as a

key stakeholder. The drive to participate in a fruitful organizational interaction with her, and the stakeholders she represented, must have been strong.

The reflection on failure is fascinating in its illustration of equal and opposite errors[16] regarding entrepreneurial activities of legitimizing. On one hand, the story illustrates how *excessive* charity to the community can be a threat to internal operations, balance sheets, and survival, and, therefore, unsustainable. Legitimizing activities can outpace internal functioning and needed resources. The company needed paying customers to meet employee wages and pay bills. Without question, material resources matter in the constitution of organizations (see Chapter 1).[8,17] We get a sense of Dee's heartsick anxiety about realizing she gave away more printing as a charitable contribution than her fledgling company had yet manufactured for paying customers. For entrepreneurial efforts more broadly, the story illustrates the danger created by imbalances among the three sets of constitutive activities for organizational constitution.

On the other hand, notice that Dee and her employees did not interpret the mishap as a reason to stop charitable giving. Refusing charity requests would have been as problematic as excessive and blind agreement to charity requests in terms of early constitution efforts. Instead, the members intuited that charitable giving was important. Of course, charitable giving is good in its own right; yet, charitable giving also serves as a legitimizing entrepreneurial activity in the sense that it promotes the perception among stakeholders that the organization is a bone fide and ethical entity worthy of continued interactions and transactions.[18]

We can read in the subtext of Dee's reflection that the discussions, which resulted in the charitable contributions policy, created a key discursive resource for public-facing representatives of the new company. The policy helped save face for members when interacting with nonprofit representatives who were asking for in-kind donations. In this way, the charitable contributions policy was the result of internal doubting-updating that helped ongoing legitimizing efforts (see Chapter 4). When interacting in the context of modern business, individuals expect that policies can and will have a "say" in their decision-making and plans. We are socialized to obey the authority of policies without much resistance or second thought.[12,19] Policy has the function of distancing the relational fallout from among interactants. Much easier to say, "Oh, because of the policy, my hands are tied," than to deny a request without reference to a faceless, impersonal policy. Otherwise, denying a request feels like an interpersonal slight. Policy justifications make denying a request much less personal and can help reduce threatening the faces of those involved.[20] Invoking policy can legitimize organizational actions by signaling we are playing by "rules of evidence and rationality" and not personal whim.[21] Thus, the crafting of the policy was a constitutive activity and afforded many other constitutive benefits. The policy proves, even presumes, we are a (legitimate) organization. Thus, Reflection 11 is an excellent example of the mutually reciprocal and interrelated nature of the subparts of the SEA model of organizationally constitutive entrepreneurial activities.

More subtly, the policy and its application to charitable contribution requestors can be seen as a multiplying activity too. Notice how news about the policy spread and eventually resulted in a queue of organized and legitimate nonprofits requesting donations of printing. Thus, we are to surmise that members of nonprofits and their boards learned about the policy and *told one another*—the legitimizing activity was multiplying perceptions of legitimacy among key stakeholders in the community.

Reflection 12: *Want to buy another business?*

"If you aren't growing, you're dying," says the business guru or sales coach. Sounds good in theory, but the devil is in the details.

During my 25 years as a business owner, I had the opportunity to buy a half a dozen other business. I did buy one, Keystone Press, which was performing well at the time of purchase, and I knew the owner (see Chapter 3, Reflection 3). The acquisition resulted in more customers, revenues, and the capacity to offer new products.

Many other opportunities came from other businesses within my franchise. They were all underperforming shops, and the owners were desperately trying to cut their losses. An underperforming company can be a good purchase. It can increase revenue and add new services. But, for an acquisition to work, out-of-pocket expenses need to be minimal. One style of deal that can work involves no upfront cash. Instead, you agree to a 10% retainer on all sales for three years. That way, both the selling owner and the buying owner are invested in the acquisition going well. That strategy can be a nice way of adding a lot of new sales and many new clients all at once. The key is to only take the sales—none of the expenses and debts. Simply fold the new customers into the existing company operations. Ideally, this kind of acquisition should be invisible to both existing and new clients.

In truth, I would have agreed to most acquisition opportunities, if I could have used that style of deal. Unfortunately, our franchise agreement did not allow it. The franchise limited these kinds of deals because they wanted physical shops to stay in place, customers to stay with shops and, of course, each physical shop to pay franchise fees.

Each time I investigated an opportunity to buy another franchise location, I concluded it was too risky. These opportunities were not in the same town as my franchise location, so an acquisition would have taken me away from my shop, which was performing well. Expenses would double, and I would need to travel to another city to build a client base. Besides those major drawbacks, the businesses for sale were always underperforming financially. I'd be taking on a lot of risk and trouble for a very small likelihood of reward.

* * *

One such opportunity came along shortly after I sold my business to my daughter, Kristi.

A shop was for sale close to her home in Kansas City.

"Mom, would you look at a store for me? Let me know whether you think it's a smart buy. It might be nice to expand the business closer to my home," she said. Because of my experience with the other franchise acquisition opportunities, she asked me to do the preliminary financial review and interview the selling owner.

I was excited for Kristi. The location could be a way for her to have a second store close to her home and boost revenues. We felt like her staff could handle her absence from her Lawrence store as she built a Kansas City client base.

The selling owner, Ralph, bought a struggling store from another owner. Ralph retired from a different career and had no experience in the printing industry. Over the years of kicking the tires on possible acquisitions, I developed a series of questions that I used to evaluate each business purchase opportunity. I sent the questions to Ralph one week before our in-person meeting, so he had time to prepare answers and documentation.

The day of the on-site visit was a mixed bag. The store was hard to find; it was in an obscure industrial area. There was no signage, only an address.

Ralph gave me a quick tour. I met his two employees and his wife. The shop was clean and organized. Also, I noted that his digital presses were new and in good shape. His press operator was pleasant and seemed competent in running the presses and performing bindery. However, his graphic designer needed an attitude adjustment.

After the tour and introductions, Ralph and I sat down in the office that he shared with his wife. He explained, "She does the books. You can ask her about the money."

"That's fine," I said, "Can we start with the questions I sent you last week and just handle them one by one?"

"Oh, well, uh, I haven't looked at those," Ralph said, side-eyeing his wife.

That told me a lot. The following are the questions that I developed after years of having to decide whether a new acquisition was worth it or whether it was merely a foolish temptation.

* * *

Question #1: What were your total sales each of the last three years?

The answer to this one ought to be easy. After a lot of side discussion between Ralph and his wife, they finally agreed that his company averaged around $250,000 in sales each of the last three years. This would be a good number for Kristi, if she could fold it into her Lawrence store. It would not be enough sales to cover his overhead and four employees. As a rule in the printing industry, $200–250,000 in annual sales is needed to support one employee. He clearly had too many employees. Most industries have these kinds of general guidelines, which can be very helpful in making quick assessments.

Questions #2 and #3: Can I review the profit and loss statements and balance sheets for the last three years?

He blamed it on his wife. She did not have time to get those done. His logic was that it did not matter because neither one of them had taken any money out of the store since buying it. That was only a small part of the information I hoped to glean from the statements. So far, the assessment was not looking good.

Question #4: Tell me about your current machinery leases and your building rental agreement.

He told me he just signed a four-year lease on two new digital printing presses. He assured me there was no problem with Kristi taking over the leases. My previous nightmare with lease agreements told me otherwise (see Chapter 4, Reflection 7). *He also admitted he just signed an extension on a building rental agreement for another 12 months.*

At this point, I was dumbfounded. I considered just ending the conversation, but I couldn't look away from this train wreck. I had to stay to see the (morbid) end.

Question #5: List your top five customers and the percent of total sales each one represents.

This is a key question. My goal was to avoid ever having my top five customers representing greater than 25% of total sales. Why? In a word, diversification. I never wanted any one customer to have that much sway over my company. Look at it like this: If five customers accounted for over 75% of the total business, the business is vulnerable to closing if one or more customers leave. That kind of customer base is just not a resilient setup.

Ultimately, Ralph refused to answer the question because he did not want to give me the names of these top customers. He was afraid I would steal them without buying his franchise. I suggested that he just give his customers' fake names to conceal their identity, along with the real proportions of total sales. That would still give me a sense of the customer base. He could not or would not produce an answer. Very fishy.

Question #6: If Kristi decides to buy this business, are you willing to introduce her personally to your top 10 customers?

The smell of fish turned to the sound of crickets. His silence was eventually followed by a meek admission. "I don't know many customers. They're all online orders and my staff handle work orders and customers," he said.

I could see that he had no working relationships with his customers—relationships that are the real value of acquiring a business. I wrapped up the conversation. I would not be recommending that Kristi consider this acquisition.

Later, I learned his company filed for bankruptcy within three months of our conversation. The franchise closed his store. He had not paid his royalties in months.

* * *

With the successful purchase of Keystone Press, we continued to look for other similar opportunities. We searched widely, beyond printing companies, to include companies that have products that we purchase from vendors. Kristi continues to watch for opportunities, such as acquiring graphic design studios, signage companies, promotional products distributors, mailing houses, and vehicle wrapping businesses.

Keep your mind open for new growth opportunities. But remember growth isn't only about building up. Tall buildings need strong foundations. Growth is great, but it needs to be done methodically. Beware of the temptation of being spread too thin.

Commentary on Reflection 12

"So you want to buy another business?" involves an inside look into deliberation around the purchase of a potential business acquisition. Kristi, a newer entrepreneur, gave Dee, Kristi's mother and an experienced entrepreneur, the task of investigating whether buying a business for sale is a good decision. The reflection illustrates the reciprocal and interdependent nature of SEA activities. On one hand, the purchase of a new acquisition could be seen as exploring activities—as with the acquisition reflection described in Chapter 3. Similarly, an active purchase of a new business could bring new customers and services with one large change, which could be construed as both legitimizing-multiplying activities, in the sense that an acquisition is growing growth that enhances stakeholders' perceptions of organizational credibility.

However, the present reflection focuses attention on the *deliberation and active decision to decline* a potential acquisition. Far from being the absence of a decision, the narrative shows how intensively Dee and Kristi decide *against* the purchase. Here, the purchase of a particular business is constructed as a threat to organizational stability and constitution—a dangerous Siren's song[22] that could upend the organization. From this vantage point, we can read their activities of investigation and deliberation as legitimizing-sustaining activities. The pair was curious about exploring the possibility of the large expansion, but curiosity was tempered by a concern that unwise growth could be de-stabilizing to the constitution of the organization.

Reflection 12 is an interesting story in the sense that the arc of the narrative concludes with *in*action. Such moments might be overlooked in terms of their constitutive power.[23] Notice how Dee's questioning of Ralph is about discerning whether the acquisition will represent a net gain or a threat to organizational constitution. Ralph's inability to answer even basic diagnostic and financial questions made it increasingly clear to Dee that the acquisition would be a burden without payoff and might even threaten the existence of Kristi's company. In the end, Dee is quick to point out that searching for opportunities is still, indeed, helpful for organizational success and expansion—points that are resonant with exploring and multiplying activities. However, the larger lesson of Reflection 12 involves sustaining activities and that growth must be smart and balanced with material demands and constraints.

Sustaining activities enact realism and avoid the dangers of naïve optimism.[24] Dee begins her story by casting the growth advice of so-called business gurus with skepticism. Taken as a whole, she neither denies the importance of growth, nor positions growth as always a desirable direction. Entrepreneurial wisdom is needed because context matters.[25] Sustaining activities, such as can be seen in careful deliberation, financial saving, and risk management, all demonstrate a careful consideration of material demands. Furthermore, sustaining activities avoid excessive and unfounded optimism about the future.[24] Storytelling of entrepreneurial sustaining activities, such as the one presented here, is rare. Such stories are antistories in that they do not lend themselves to heroic plotlines,[10] but, instead, to the workaday action and deliberation in which wise options are accepted and protected and unwise options are avoided.[24]

Legitimizing-sustaining are a set of entrepreneurial activities because *un*sustainable growth represents an ongoing threat to being seen as legitimate in the eyes of important stakeholders. When growth outpaces other constitutive activities, such as those of internal operations (see Chapter 4), then the organization itself will begin to degrade and falter. Imagine how taking on more financial burden in terms of loan payments can create a situation in which loans move to default, creditors repossess equipment, landlords evict, employee wages are not paid, and so forth. Slow—or fast-moving—decline in key stakeholders' perceptions that the organization exists and is a good faith interactional and transactional partner can fail. In turn, so too will organizational constitution. Indeed, sustaining activities may not be the stuff of popular motivational business speakers, but they are certainly crucial to entrepreneurship that requires long-term organizational constitution.

Conclusion

This chapter described the third set of entrepreneurial activities in the SEA model, which involve the constitution of external stakeholder perceptions and interactions. Legitimizing-multiplying/ sustaining activities are needed so that stakeholders perceive the organization as a bona fide and desirable interaction partner. Without such efforts, the value propositions which motivate the need for organization will, at best, remain a vision or idea but will not result in needed perceptions and resources flowing into the organization. The autobiographical reflections offered in this chapter point to the diverse and context-sensitive ways legitimizing-multiplying/sustaining activities occur. Without these activities, organization constitution itself will not be present definitionally, will fade, or decline.

Notes

1 See page 27 in Pfeffer, J. (2009). Understanding power in organizations. In D. Tjosvold, & B. Wisse (Eds.), *Power and interdependence in organizations* (pp. 17–32). Cambridge: Cambridge University Press.
2 McPhee, R. D., & Zaug, P. (2000). The communicative constitution of organizations: A framework for explanation. *Electronic Journal of Communication, 10*(1 and 2), 1–16.
3 McPhee, R. D., & Iverson, J. (2009). Agents of constitution in the communidad: Constitutive processes of communication in organizations. In L. L. Putnam, & A. M. Nicotera (Eds.), *Building theories of organization: The constitutive role of communication* (pp. 49–88). New York: Routledge.
4 Bisel, R. S. (2010). A communicative ontology of organization? A description, history, and critique of CCO theories for organization science. *Management Communication Quarterly, 24*(1), 124–131. doi:10.1177/0893318909351582.
5 Gupta, V. K., Turban, D. B., Wasti, S. A., & Sikdar, A. (2009). The role of gender stereotypes in perceptions of entrepreneurs and intentions to become an entrepreneur. *Entrepreneurship Theory and Practice, 33*(2), 397–417.
6 Stead, V. (2017). Belonging and women entrepreneurs: Women's navigation of gendered assumptions in entrepreneurial practice. *International Small Business Journal: Researching Entrepreneurship, 35*(1), 61–77. doi:10.1177/0266242615594413.
7 Long, Z., & Buzzanell, P. M. (2021). Constituting intersectional politics of reinscription: Women entrepreneurs' resistance practices in China, Denmark, and the United States. *Management Communication Quarterly.* doi:10.1177/08933189211030246.
8 Bruscella, J. S., & Bisel, R. S. (2018). Four flows theory and materiality: ISIL's use of material resources in its communicative constitution. *Communication Monographs, 85*(3), 331–356. doi:10.1080/03637751.2017.1420907.
9 Hull, M. S. (2012). Documents and bureaucracy. *Annual Review of Anthropology, 41*, 251–267. doi:10.1146/annurev.anthro.012809.104953.
10 Bisel, R. S., Fairhurst, G. T., & Sheep, M. L. (2022). CCO theory and leadership. In J. Basque, N. Bencherki, & T. Kuhn (Eds.), *Routledge handbook of CCO* (pp. 297–309). New York: Routledge.
11 O'Connor, A., & Shumate, M. (2018). A multidimensional network approach to strategic communication. *International Journal of Strategic Communication, 12*(4), 399–416. doi:10.1080/1553118X.2018.1452242.

12 Koschmann, M. A., & McDonald, J. (2015). Organizational rituals, communication, and the question of agency. *Management Communication Quarterly, 29*(2), 229–256. doi:10.1177/0893318915572386.

13 Cooren, F. (2006). The organizational world as a plenum of agencies. In J. R. T. Cooren, & E. J. Van Every (Eds.), *Communication as organizing: Empirical and theoretical explorations in the dynamic of text and conversation* (pp. 81–100). Mahwah, NJ: Erlbaum.

14 Taylor, J. R., & Cooren, F. (1997). What makes communication 'organizational'? How the many voices of a collectivity become the one voice of an organization. *Journal of Pragmatics, 27*, 409–438. doi:10.1016/S0378-2166(96)00044-6.

15 Granovetter, M. S. (1973). The strength of weak ties. *American Journal of Sociology, 78*, 1360–1380.

16 Lewis, C. S. (2001). *The screwtape letters*. Grand Rapids, MI: Zondervan.

17 Ashcraft, K. L., Kuhn, T. R., & Cooren, F. (2009). Constitutional amendments: "Materializing" organizational communication. *Academy of Management Annals, 3*, 1–64. doi:10.5465/19416520903047186.

18 Bisel, R. S. (2017). *Organizational moral learning: A communication approach*. New York: Routledge.

19 Weber, M. (1924/1978). *Economy and society: An outline of interpretive sociology: Vol. 1*. Berkeley: University of California Press.

20 Bisel, R. S., & Kramer, M. W. (2014). Denying what workers believe are unethical workplace requests: Do workers use moral, operational, or policy justifications publicly? *Management Communication Quarterly, 28*(1), 111–129. doi:10.1177/0893318913503382.

21 See p. 369 in Brown, R. H. (1978). Bureaucracy as praxis: Toward a political phenomenology of formal organizations. *Administrative Science Quarterly, 23*, 365–382. doi:10.2307/2392415.

22 Palmer, G. H. (Trans.) (1999). *Homer: The Odyssey*. New York: Dover.

23 Wood, M. S., Williams, D. W., & Drover, W. (2017). Past as prologue: Entrepreneurial inaction decisions and subsequent action judgments. *Journal of Business Venturing, 32*(1), 107–127. doi:10.1016/j.jbusvent.2016.10.008.

24 Trevelyan, R. (2008). Optimism, overconfidence and entrepreneurial activity. *Management Decision, 46*, 986–1001. doi:10.1108/00251740810890177.

25 Dunham, L., McVea, J., & Freeman, R. E. (2008). Entrepreneurial wisdom: Incorporating the ethical and strategic dimensions of entrepreneurial decision-making. *International Journal of Entrepreneurship and Small Business, 6*(1), 8–19.

Index

Printed in the United States
by Baker & Taylor Publisher Services